That one line—the Spirit led Jesus int[...]
be tempted by the devil—haunts me. And yet in these
pages, I'm invited to follow, too, further into this terrifying,
merciful terrain. Probing both Scripture and our soul's
story, Brown unfolds how our elder brother descended into
the wilderness we all must enter and confronted the primal
questions that lurk in the secret places of our heart. Here is
a wise and gentle pen, providing ancient, sturdy wisdom as
balm to every human longing.

**WINN COLLIER,** director of the Eugene Peterson Center for Christian
Imagination, author of *A Burning in My Bones* and *Love Big, Be Well*

Brown writes, "In my suffering, I came to understand
that sometimes we experience God's power through his
protection, but in a broken world, sometimes we experience
God's power through his consolation." These words are not
quick fixes and don't offer fake escape. Instead, *The Ache for
Meaning* gives us a refreshing spaciousness in suffering and
offers an invitation to move more fully into people of faith
living in the ordinary hard of life. Brown brings realistic,
clear, and grounded hope and reminds us that Jesus meets
us right where we are.

**SARA BILLUPS,** author of *Orphaned Believers*

Like a scalpel, a good question has the power to cut to
the quick, exposing the sicknesses that lie just beneath the
surface of our lives. And like a skilled surgeon, Tommy
Brown leverages that most cryptic and evocative of Gospel

texts, the temptation of Christ, to show how the questions posed to Christ are in fact *our* questions—*Will I have enough? Am I enough? Do I matter?* In so doing, he exposes the lies, fears, compulsions, and contradictions that might otherwise drive our lives into ruin to the gaze of the Healer. A wise and much-needed book.

ANDREW ARNDT, pastor of New Life East, author of *All Flame* and *Streams in the Wasteland*

Tommy Brown understands the kind of questions about meaning that many of us ponder. I enjoyed his blend of disarmingly honest personal stories, insightful wisdom about Christian identity, and creative engagement with Jesus' three temptations. Brown has a Christ-centered understanding of power and control that will challenge readers, and I appreciate his suggestions for spiritual practices to address the issues raised by each temptation. I was sad when I got to the end of the book—I was so enjoying pondering questions of identity and meaning along with him.

REV. DR. LYNNE M. BAAB, author of *Sabbath Keeping* and *Joy Together*

In this personal and engaging book, Tommy Brown uses the temptation of Christ to wrestle deeply with three of life's most important questions: *Will I have enough? Am I enough? Do I matter?* Throughout he sheds new light on Scripture and offers much wisdom for us to live more virtuous lives. Highly recommend!

DR. CHRISTIAN B. MILLER, A. C. Reid Professor of Philosophy at Wake Forest University

Each section of Tommy Brown's book opens with a question that every one of us ponders deeply and out of the sight of others: *Will I have enough? Am I enough? Do I matter?* Tommy opens his own life to reveal how he has struggled to answer each of these questions and then leads us not only to see the invitations Jesus extends to help us answer these questions but also to engage in practices that allow us to say yes to these invitations. You will be encouraged in that deep, lasting way after reading Tommy's book, and your perspective will expand so that you really begin to embrace the security, worth, and belovedness you have in Christ.

**KELLYE FABIAN STORY**, writer, lawyer, pastor, cultural observer, and author of *Sacred Questions* and *Holy Vulnerability*

Weaving personal and real-life stories into thoughtful reflections on Jesus in the Gospels, Tommy Brown helps us reimagine the temptation of Jesus around the fundamental issues of our identity—issues surrounding security, approval, and power. This kind of spiritual reading of the temptations gives us the opportunity to enter more fully into the virtues of trust, gratitude, and meekness that we might become more like Jesus. Tommy is a faithful pastor and guide, providing practices that ground readers in each of these virtues. *The Ache for Meaning* is a compelling invitation for self-reflection and growth into Christlikeness.

**DEREK VREELAND**, pastor and author of *Centering Jesus*

We don't all get there at the same time, but boy howdy we all get there, to that stifling wilderness moment, maybe even season, when whatever money and success and power and influence we've accrued feel achingly empty. It's a classic case of getting the course before the heart—not so much *what* needs we have but *how* we try and meet them. With pastoral wit and wisdom, Tommy Brown's *The Ache for Meaning* mines the riches in the wilderness temptations of Christ. The three questions Jesus faced and the subsequent responses he gave provide life-saving guidance for anyone high-centered in the wilderness. For we all get there, boy howdy we do.

**JOHN BLASE**, poet and author

# THE ACHE FOR
# MEANING

*How the Temptations of Christ Reveal*

*Who We Are and What We're Seeking*

## TOMMY BROWN

A NavPress resource published in alliance
with Tyndale House Publishers

NavPress is the publishing ministry of The Navigators, an international Christian organization and leader in personal spiritual development. NavPress is committed to helping people grow spiritually and enjoy lives of meaning and hope through personal and group resources that are biblically rooted, culturally relevant, and highly practical.

**For more information, visit NavPress.com.**

*The Ache for Meaning: How the Temptations of Christ Reveal Who We Are and What We're Seeking*

Copyright © 2023 by Respokin. All rights reserved.

A NavPress resource published in alliance with Tyndale House Publishers

*NavPress* and the NavPress logo are registered trademarks of NavPress, The Navigators, Colorado Springs, CO. *Tyndale* is a registered trademark of Tyndale House Ministries. Absence of ® in connection with marks of NavPress or other parties does not indicate an absence of registration of those marks.

The Team:
David Zimmerman, Publisher; Caitlyn Carlson, Acquisitions Editor; Elizabeth Schroll, Copy Editor; Olivia Eldredge, Operations Manager; Ron C. Kaufmann, Designer; Sarah K. Johnson, Proofreading Coordinator

Cover image of Jesus' temptation copyright © CSA Images/iStockphoto. All rights reserved.

Author photograph copyright © 2021 by Sheena Ratliff, and used with permission.

Published in association with The Bindery Agency, www.TheBinderyAgency.com

Scripture quotations are from The ESV® Bible (The Holy Bible, English Standard Version®), copyright © 2001 by Crossway, a publishing ministry of Good News Publishers. Used by permission. All rights reserved. Scripture quotations marked NIV are from the Holy Bible, New International Version,® NIV.® Copyright © 1973, 1978, 1984, 2011 by Biblica, Inc.® Used by permission. All rights reserved worldwide.

Some of the anecdotal illustrations in this book are true to life and are included with the permission of the persons involved. All other illustrations are composites of real situations, and any resemblance to people living or dead is purely coincidental.

For information about special discounts for bulk purchases, please contact Tyndale House Publishers at csresponse@tyndale.com, or call 1-855-277-9400.

ISBN 978-1-64158-627-6

Printed in the United States of America

| 29 | 28 | 27 | 26 | 25 | 24 | 23 |
|----|----|----|----|----|----|----|
| 7  | 6  | 5  | 4  | 3  | 2  | 1  |

*To Kevin Frack*

# Contents

*Everywhere is desert.*

THOMAS MERTON,

*Thoughts in Solitude*

# THE THREE QUESTIONS
# WE'VE ALWAYS ASKED

I REPEATEDLY REARRANGED my office at work. I tried new places for the desk—back wall, over to the left, across to the right. And then there were the chairs. Should I position them in front of my desk, or perhaps in the corner with a table between? One felt too formal; the other not formal enough. Over and again, I rearranged my office, not sure what I was looking for or what was missing. All I knew was that I hoped shuffling furniture would spark creativity, or at least a desire to show up to that space and do work I no longer found meaningful.

The company had provided nice furniture for our offices, but it was fake nice—engineered wood with a polished surface that crumbles when cracked.

That wood felt like a mirror.

From outward appearances, all was well with me, but beneath the surface, fissures expanded. So often I felt out of place in this corporate world. The power dynamics were disorienting, and I could rarely figure out where I stood. Just when I felt secure, something would happen that shook my confidence. I knew something was wrong, but I had no idea where to begin to make it right.

You can only rearrange furniture so many ways before you must face the possibility that the problem is not a lack of feng shui. My problem was that I was seeking answers to questions I could not name. Deep questions, embedded somewhere indiscernible in my soul, leaving me longing to resolve my uneasiness and unfulfillment.

I'd hoped my current job would infuse my life with meaning and answer these questions for me. The job before that, I'd wanted my mentor-boss to answer them for me. The job before that, I'd wanted my accomplishments to answer them for me. Every try, every grasp for meaning, every flailing search for solid ground—nothing was enough.

Here I was, nearly forty years old, and not only did I not have the answers, but I couldn't even ask the questions that haunted me inside that fake-furniture office.

+ +

The indefinable ache, the longing, the unspoken and unnamed need—it's part of the human condition. We know we're looking for something, but we don't know what it is.

We might know how we got to where we are, but we don't know what to do next.

There's a story in Genesis where the Lord promises an elderly, childless man named Abram that he will have countless offspring.[1] A decade later, he remains childless, and his wife, Sarai, proposes that Abram sleep with her servant, Hagar, which he does.

Hagar becomes pregnant, and animosity simmers between her and Sarai, who now has what she wants but doesn't want what she has.[2] Under duress, Hagar flees into the wilderness, stopping to rest at a spring.

An angel finds her and asks, "Where have you come from and where are you going?"

Hagar responds, "I am fleeing from . . ."

She knows where she's come from, but she doesn't know where she's going.

Before I worked in my fake-furniture office, I was a pastor. I wasn't the *real* pastor, as some enjoyed reminding me. I was the person the real pastor hires to do the day-to-day operational stuff. Some thrive doing this type of ministerial work. It suffocated my sense of calling.

The challenge was, I was good at it. I created so many systems and programs and oversaw so many employees that I was very useful—indispensable, some said—to the church. But being useful was using up my best energies.

I grew to resent the church because much of what I was doing had nothing to do with the things that I felt called to do—things like preaching, teaching, and providing spiritual guidance. I had grown so focused on being useful and helping others accomplish what they wanted that I'd become disconnected from what it was that I wanted. After all, I'd seen what happens when pastors aren't useful—they're asked to *find the will of God somewhere else.* The thought of income loss, of not making ends meet, seemed like a fate worse than death. This fearful grasping for safety, for having enough, wore me down. Eventually, the responsibilities on my job description as a pastor proved to be the gravest challenge to my calling to, in fact, *be* a pastor.

Wearied, I told my boss that I'd lost my way and I needed a change, that I needed to reclaim a sense of doing and being what I was called to do and be. So I left the church and went to work for the company with the fake office furniture.

On some level, I didn't want to leave the church. I loved the people with whom I worked and those in the congregation, but I knew I couldn't get clarity if I remained.

I was fleeing, and though I knew the location of my new office, I had no idea where I was actually going.

+

Sometimes I went for slow jogs. I was suffering from anxiety, which had never really plagued me before, and I'd heard that exercise helped.

But there was one problem—my head was still attached to my slow-jogging body. And I was out on a trail without my convenient distractions: books, problems to solve, dopamine hits from social media—all the things that could momentarily soothe my anxious mind.

I'd heard that meditation helped. So I tried to meditate, but I ended up ruminating on more things to be anxious about.

Most of the things that should have helped ended up making me feel even more defeated.

I found only one space where my mind was focused and calm. In my study at home, I could put a song on repeat and open my laptop and write—and I was good for hours, fully absorbed in the moment, even to the point of forgetting to eat until dinnertime.

This one practice became a haven. Even though day by day I had to leave this space and rearrange my fake-furniture office, it felt like here all the furniture of my mind was in its proper place.

One morning in my study, the questions I could not name began to whisper in words that I could faintly discern. It was like they were finally ready to be seen, ready to be named.

As I sat at my solid-wood desk, by the window overlooking a row of mature junipers, I opened the Bible.

To knock the religious edges off this moment: You should know that there were no goose bumps, no sense of Divine Presence—nothing surreal. Just me at my desk, opening the book I'd opened countless times before.

When you've been trained as a pastor, it's part of the territory to know the Scriptures. You spend untold hours with this book, and eventually the stories become familiar. Familiarity, I'm told, breeds unfamiliarity, and unfamiliarity breeds contempt.[3] I hadn't devolved into contempt for Scripture, but at best I had become so familiar with it that it hardly intrigued me.

The Scripture I opened to that day had worn thin to transparency after years of sermons. But this time, in this place, with rare silence of mind, something happened.

*Sometimes when
you read the Bible,
the Bible reads you.*

Then Jesus came from Galilee to the Jordan to John, to be baptized by him. John would have prevented him, saying, "I need to be baptized by you, and do you come to me?" But Jesus answered him, "Let it be so now, for thus it is fitting for us to fulfill all righteousness." Then he consented. And when Jesus was baptized, immediately he went up from the water, and behold, the heavens were opened to him, and he saw the Spirit of God descending like a dove and coming to rest on him; and behold, a voice from heaven said, "This is my beloved Son, with whom I am well pleased."

Then Jesus was led up by the Spirit into the wilderness to be tempted by the devil. And after fasting forty days and forty nights, he was hungry. And the tempter came and said to him, "If you are the Son of God, command these stones to become loaves of bread." But he answered, "It is written,

"'Man shall not live by bread alone,
but by every word that comes from the mouth
of God.'"

Then the devil took him to the holy city and set him on the pinnacle of the temple and said to him, "If you are the Son of God, throw yourself down, for it is written,

"'He will command his angels concerning you,'

and

"'On their hands they will bear you up,
      lest you strike your foot against a stone.'"

Jesus said to him, "Again it is written, 'You shall not put the Lord your God to the test.'" Again, the devil took him to a very high mountain and showed him all the kingdoms of the world and their glory. And he said to him, "All these I will give you, if you will fall down and worship me." Then Jesus said to him, "Be gone, Satan! For it is written,

"'You shall worship the Lord your God
      and him only shall you serve.'"

Then the devil left him, and behold, angels came and were ministering to him.

Slowly, devils leave.

As I sat in my study and read Christ's temptations, emotions welled within me. I was reading the words written on a page in front of me, but the words were speaking to the deep questions written on my soul.

I wept.

I wept for a long time.

I wept for lost time.

I wept like I imagine Hagar weeping, running as far and as fast as she can from pain, knowing what she is running from but not what or where she is running to.

Then, in all that running from something, she runs smack into the divine.

And she says, "Would I have looked here for the one who sees me?"[4]

There's something about being seen—about knowing that you're not alone and that you matter—that fills you with hope, even if you're not yet out of the woods. Sometimes this happens in ways you never would have expected. Amid all my pain and longing, as I gazed on Christ's temptations, I was shocked to catch a glimpse of what I was really seeking.

I found my deepest fears and greatest hopes on that page. As I read of the devil tempting Jesus to abandon his identity, I was confronted with my most debased instincts and my most primal passions.

And suddenly, this scene was everywhere, all the time. I began to hear echoes from Jesus' wilderness temptations[5] in conversations I was having, in challenges I was facing. As I returned to this story over and over, I also saw my questions with greater clarity.

I found a whole new way to see the world.

And once you see, you can't unsee.

This passage of Scripture felt like an invitation to a journey of exploring my questions, and through my questions, what it was I was truly seeking.

*Journey* is such an overplayed word, but I can't find a better one to describe the path that this passage set me on—a path I've walked for many years now and one that I'll continue to follow. It's a transformational journey, one of learning to walk in contentment, fulfillment, and hope.

Some journeys are about destinations. I quickly discerned that this one was not. This journey was about Invitations— invitations to explore the questions that began to shape who I was and what I was seeking. As the poet Rilke encouraged, you must live these sorts of questions.[6] The point isn't to quickly find a correct answer; the point is to experience transformation as you live with the questions in the foreground of your heart and mind. And eventually, in living them well, the questions become a sort of answer in themselves.

As I lived the questions, I realized that the frustration I felt as a pastor and the meaninglessness I felt in the fake-furniture office were because none of the answers I'd been given could guide me through this wilderness I was wandering.

> When all the answers failed, the questions guided me home.

Money couldn't buy the security I needed.

Success couldn't provide the approval I desired.

Power and control corroded my soul.

But when all the answers failed, the questions guided me home.

The passage about Jesus' temptations, which doesn't contain even one question, revealed to me my questions, the places in my soul that longed to be noticed. While you could express these three questions in different ways, this is how I saw them, and how I see them still:

- *Will I have enough?*
- *Am I enough?*
- *Do I matter?*

As I considered the questions over time, as I conversed with friends and provided spiritual guidance for others, I realized these aren't just *my* questions. These are *our* questions—they echo in every human soul. And though we're all asking these three questions in different ways, we hardly—if ever—voice them.

Because if we asked these questions aloud, we'd risk vulnerability.

And vulnerability opens us to the possibility of rejection.

But vulnerability also opens us to the possibility of solidarity.

And solidarity means we're not alone.

It means *you're* not alone.

You can trust that we're all seeking the same things, asking the same three questions in one form or another. The most personal desires are the most universal, and the most universal desires are the most personal.[7]

And the most ancient.

These three questions drove the plot that led to tragedy in the Garden with Adam and Eve. They're the questions Abraham faced on his trek to Mount Moriah to sacrifice his son Isaac. They're the same ones Moses and Israel experienced during their wilderness wanderings.

Suffice it to say that once you see the questions, you'll see them in some form in chapter after chapter of Scripture.

And you'll see them in every chapter of your life. As author Fyodor Dostoevsky wrote of the wilderness temptations in his novel *The Brothers Karamazov*,

> For in these three questions all of subsequent human
> history is as if brought together into a single whole
> and foretold; three images are revealed that will
> take in all the insoluble historical contradictions of
> human nature over all the earth.[8]

In other words, the three temptations Jesus faced represent every temptation you will face in life, every temptation humankind has ever faced. They are the three areas where each of us is tempted to meet healthy human needs in unhealthy ways.

Spiritual director and teacher Ruth Haley Barton explains:

The mind works hard to control and manage reality and has its own plans for remedying the human situation outside of Christ and abandonment to his divine will. Thomas Keating, in his work on the true self and the false, describes these plans as "emotional programs for happiness" based on childhood instinctual needs and all the ways we compensate for these unfulfilled needs. He identifies these basic, primal impulses as the following needs:

- safety/security/survival
- affection/esteem/approval
- power and control

All of these are legitimate human needs. The sin problem has to do with the fact that we have all developed unconscious ways of meeting these needs for ourselves on our own terms . . . apart from God.[9]

With each temptation, the devil invited Jesus to meet a healthy need—security, approval, or control—on his own terms and in his own power. I love pastor and theologian Eugene Peterson's take on what transpired:

The devil's three temptations of Jesus all had to do with ways and means. Every one of the devil's goals was excellent. The devil had an unsurpassed vision statement. But the ways and means were incompatible with the ends. Jesus saw through it at once.[10]

*The issue was not what needs Jesus had but how he would meet them. The same applies to us.*

The issue was not *what* needs Jesus had but *how* he would meet them. The same applies to us.

We'll explore the depths of these questions and temptations— and what God has for us in them—throughout the coming chapters. But before we're too far along the trail, I want us to understand the big picture of what's happening in each of the three Temptations:[11]

- The first temptation—turn these stones into bread (Matthew 4:3)—addresses the first question: *Will I have enough?* It's the temptation to strive for security. It's based in the fear that we will not have enough, which causes us to seek security in our own efforts and abilities to produce, provide, and make something happen. This temptation leads us away from contentment.

- The second temptation—throw yourself down from the Temple (Matthew 4:5-6)—addresses the second question: *Am I enough?* Here's the temptation to perform for approval. It's based in the belief that we do not measure up, which causes us to burn immense energy and resources to impress others, keep up appearances, and gain approval. This temptation leads us away from fulfillment.

- The third temptation—bow down and worship (Matthew 4:9)—addresses the third question: *Do I matter?* Here we see the seduction to exercise power to control. It's based in our search for significance, which causes us to seek unhealthy control over people, positions, and problems. This temptation leads us away from hope in God alone.

We're in this together, asking the same three questions, facing the same three temptations, trying to meet the same three needs in one form or another. To begin our journey, we'll discover how Jesus' sense of identity gave him the strength to stand in the face of adversity. Then we'll unpack the Temptations one by one:

- exploring the core need and question each temptation exposes;
- understanding the mindset that Jesus possessed, allowing him to resist each temptation; and
- developing an ancient spiritual practice that Jesus performed to strengthen this mindset.

My commitment to you is that I'll offer guidance by only speaking of what I've personally experienced as true and helpful. And while I can't say everything that needs to be said about any one topic, I'll leave nothing off the table that has led to personal renewal.

This transformational journey can change your heart and help you become a more joyful, liberated, and confident person. These are not empty promises; these are invitations to become more like Jesus—the One who showed us what it means to be truly human.

Before long, you'll learn to look at any situation and ask yourself, *What valid need—security, approval, or control—am I trying to meet in an unhealthy way and on my own terms?* You'll begin to discern which of the three core questions—which of the three temptations, that is—you're facing.

How far you take this journey is up to you. Just know that you'll never arrive at a place where you feel like you've mastered much of anything in the spiritual life, because when it comes to following the Master, we are all novices.

As you see Christ's wilderness temptations take shape in various forms in your daily life and interactions, you'll awaken to the reality that everywhere is wilderness, and we're all walking in it.

But we're not walking alone.

If we're listening, if our inner ears are attuned to what the Spirit is doing and saying, we'll hear echoes from Christ's temptations that show us who we are and what we're seeking. And in the end, perhaps we'll not only hear the echoes from the Temptations but also the Voice that reminds us, as it reminded him, that we are beloved sons and daughters of God.

Now, into the wilderness.

# THE FOUNDATION
# OF IDENTITY

SOME EXPERIENCES SEND ME BACK to childhood. The scent of fresh-cut grass calls to mind the golf course where I worked as a teenager. Rustling fall leaves remind me of hours in the woods hunting with my father. A melody calls forth a memory. A passing stranger reminds me of my deceased grandmother, Rebecca.

Like sights, smells, and sounds, words—and the stories they compose—evoke memories.

To be a Jewish boy in Jesus' generation was to have your mind filled, your imagination shaped, and your character forged by your ancestors' stories—the stories of Scripture. Just as in our modern world, where if you sing the opening line of a popular song, others can easily finish it, in Jesus' day, even the faintest reference to a familiar Scripture story led to the drama of that story unfolding in a well-trained Jewish mind. Given his role as not just a casual student of Scripture but as one who became a rabbi, Jesus knew all the stories by heart. Start the story; he could finish it.

So it was with his temptations.

The temptations Jesus faced were not the devil's inventions. They were based in Scripture stories Jesus recognized—iconic moments from Israel's history that represented all other temptations that Israel ever faced. Whereas you and I might not pick up the backstory when reading the Temptations, Jesus was dialed in to the deeper significance from the tempter's first phrase.

As he faced his first temptation, Jesus recalled how the people of Israel grumbled about not having food while wandering the wilderness (Exodus 16), and with his second, when they tested God at Massah (Exodus 17), and in his third, when they worshiped the golden calf at Mount Sinai (Exodus 32).

As each temptation was unveiled, and with it each memory from Israel's history, the atmosphere grew thick with tension and heavy with significance. Jesus understood that there was more at stake than passing three random tests. These specific tests were designed to prove his personal faithfulness to God as God's Son.[1] And as the Son of God, given the meaning and importance of this title in his world, he knew that he also represented his people, the Israelites, who were also referred to as God's son in Scripture.[2] Where they had failed, would he succeed?

One can only imagine the emotions Jesus felt as the three temptations shrouded him like a gathering storm. It hadn't been all that long since he'd emerged from the Jordan River, hair dripping with baptismal water, mind brimming with God's good words. But now, amid soul-bruising darkness and intense pressure, all this was called into question. Jesus was forced to grapple with what it meant to be the person the Voice declared him to be—the Son of God.

✛

When I was a boy, my grandfather Blain told my younger brother, Chris, and me, "If one of you ever gets into a fight and I hear that the other didn't jump in to help, I'm going to wear you out." Allow me to translate Southern vernacular: He was going to spank us. Now, he never did, because we never got into a fight, but his point was clear: Since you are brothers, look out for each other. This is what was expected of a boy in our family.

Something is lost in translation in Jesus' temptations, and we need to get it sorted. The tempter's words to Jesus, "If you are the Son of God," may also be translated as "*Since* you are the Son of God."[3] Like my grandfather challenging my brother and me with what it meant to be a boy in our family, the devil challenged Jesus to prove his sonship and validate his calling as the chosen one of Israel.

Now we can see the devil's strategy from a new angle:

*Since you are the Son of God, prove it. Show us how the Son of God acts. Meet your own needs in your own way by turning stones to bread. Dazzle, amaze, and garner approval as you leap from the Temple into angel arms. Rescue your people, gain control, and rule with absolute power in the face of your oppressors and opponents. This is what people expect from the Son of God. Since you are the Son of God, you should do these things.*

Perhaps as you face temptations, the stakes don't seem quite as high. But surely you can relate. Since you are a woman or man, look and act and behave *this* way. Since you are a wife, mother, father, husband, grandparent, widow, Christian, boss, pastor, stay-at-home parent, administrative assistant, teacher, teenager, young adult, student, athlete, or whatever label among countless labels you've been given or claimed, you must measure up, step up, and meet expectations—since you are what you are.

We're all tempted to conform to the patterns of this world[4] because we all have a deep-seated need to know that we will be secure and approved of and have some control over our lives. But these pathways to happiness that we're offered inevitably fail, and we find ourselves anxious, unfulfilled, or in despair. This happens because the deepest part of us knows who we truly are, what we long to be, and what we really seek.

Your true self, the Christlike essence of your being, longs to emerge.[5] But it won't if you're following the paths that the Temptations seduce you to follow. These paths, wide and well worn though they are, are not safe for your soul—so your true self remains hidden, and your deepest needs persist unfulfilled.

There is a path that leads to contentment, fulfillment, and hope, but you're not going to stumble your way onto it. The gate is narrow, and the way is hard, but it leads to eternal life.[6] Walking it will take intentionality, discernment, and practice. Anyone who tells you there are instant and easy ways to true spiritual growth and maturity is deceived, sincere though they may be. They're offering you shadows of the good and true and beautiful life you're seeking. Like Satan's temptations to Jesus, they're offering you shortcuts that lead to ruin.

*Your true self, the Christlike essence of your being, longs to emerge.*

Your soul's true path is "a long obedience in the same direction."[7] There are no shortcuts. It's a lifelong path that leads to ongoing awakening to who you truly are—a child of God.

This is the reason we must see what's really happening in Jesus' responses to each temptation, how he met his deepest needs, and the mindsets and practices that kept him faithful to his vocation as God's Son.

In your Bible, the temptation story in Matthew is likely marked with a heading that states something like "The Temptation of Jesus," perhaps followed by the words of Matthew 4:1: "Then

Jesus was led up by the Spirit into the wilderness to be tempted by the devil." But this isn't where the temptation narrative really begins, because you can't understand what happens in the wilderness unless you understand what transpired at the river. It's all connected—one seamless event.

At the Jordan River, when Jesus was baptized by his cousin John, the heavens opened, the Spirit descended like a dove, and a voice declared, "This is my beloved Son, with whom I am well pleased."[8] This—Jesus' baptism—is the beginning of the temptation scene. Before he's driven by the Spirit into the wilderness to be tested, he's baptized in the river and hears the Voice of God affirming him.

Now, as powerful and meaningful as these words were in and of themselves, the timing of when they were spoken was also of utmost importance: God the Father proclaimed this reality *before* Jesus faced his tests, not *because* he passed them.

As a father, I know the power of encouraging words to uplift the soul. I've coached my son Seth's baseball team several times. I love watching him put on his helmet and stroll to the plate. I often position myself as a base coach, which means I sometimes have a moment to speak to him as he strides toward the batter's box.

He's a great athlete, but I never want Seth to think that my affirmation and admiration of him are based on his performance. So I'll often pull him aside before he hits and tell him, "I want you to have fun up there. Give it your absolute best effort, and whatever happens, I'm your biggest fan. I love you, Son."

Sometimes Seth jogs back to the dugout and passes me after hitting a home run; sometimes he passes after striking out. Nothing changes about our relationship based on his performance. Sure, if he continually struggles, we'll tweak some of his mechanics; we always seek to improve. But my love for him transcends anything he could ever do or not do. Seth has nothing to prove that would have an impact on him being my son.

He'll be my son all his life, and there is nothing he can do to change this reality.

Like Seth striding toward the plate having heard encouraging words from his father, Jesus enters the wilderness to face his temptations in full confidence as his Father's beloved, well-pleasing Son. And he does this having not passed one test, performed one miracle, or preached one sermon.

So when Jesus faces what the enemy throws at him, when he's tempted to prove his sonship, his Father's words echo through his mind: *This is my beloved Son, with whom I am well pleased.*

Though much is on the line, there's nothing for Jesus to prove regarding his sonship. He only needs to remain faithful to what he knows to be true about himself, about his Father, and about how he as the Son should trust and obey his Father.

In this moment and for the rest of his life—throughout

all his ministry and miracles and teachings—Jesus' identity flows *from* his Father's words of approval, not *for* his Father's words of approval. So when the devil says, "Since you are the Son of God" *do this or that*, Jesus doesn't feel the need to prove himself. He understands who he is, and he doesn't need to deviate from the identity and assignment his Father has given him to prove anything.

This ability to receive, embrace, and live from a God-given sense of identity has profound implications for our lives as well, because as scandalous as this might seem, it's breathtakingly true—what God says about Jesus, God says about you. You are God's beloved child. And what God says about you is not based on your momentary performance, good or bad. It's based in the unshakable, unfathomable love of God for his children, for all who believe and receive him.[9] It's based in God's kindness, God's unmerited grace, and God's belief in the potential of each one of us when we claim our identity as his beloved son or daughter.

> *Jesus' identity flows from his Father's words of approval, not for his Father's words of approval.*

We know that sometimes we will strike out, miss the mark, and not achieve our potential. Nevertheless, we can remain confident in our identity as our Father's beloved children—not by our own merit but because of the Father's love. And in a mystery that transcends anything we could possibly wrap our brains around, our identity as beloved sons and daughters is because of what Christ did for us—including how he faced his temptations, lived his life, died his death, and was raised to life again.

> Jesus' obedience, his living out his identity as the beloved Son of God, becomes our invitation, inspiration, and empowerment to fulfill the destinies that the Father has for each of us.

His obedience, his living out his identity as the beloved Son of God, becomes our invitation, inspiration, and empowerment to fulfill the destinies that the Father has for each of us.

But like Jesus, if we're going to face our everyday temptations and live into the fullness of who we can become, we must embrace the life-giving words that God has spoken over our lives: that we are God's beloved children, with whom God is well pleased. In these words we find the answers to our deepest questions.

# Will I Have Enough?

# TEMPTATION:
# STRIVE FOR SECURITY

IN THE SUMMER OF 2014, a few colleagues and I spent a week at a Jewish retreat center. One afternoon, our hosts instructed us to change into swimwear, grab a towel, and board the bed of the farm's old pickup. They told us we were heading to the river, but that was all the information they gave.

As paved roads devolved into dirt trails, we arrived at a clearing in a field, the river a half mile away. We sprinted like children through thigh-high weeds toward the river's bank. Our Jewish friends outpaced my small cohort of Christian men, arriving first at the water's edge.

When I finally arrived and joined the group, I took a minute to catch my breath—hands on knees, pulse pounding.

Eventually I lifted my head and stood upright—and was startled to behold our guides stripping down to their birthday suits and wading into the water.

Unnerved, I lowered my head and stared at my flip-flopped feet, my swimming trunks firmly in place as others slipped nude and knee-deep into the river.

"We're here for a mikvah," said our guide as he stood downstream. "It's a ritual cleansing to prepare for Sabbath, where we immerse ourselves in flowing water."

He continued, "As we stand in this river, with the water careening toward us, coursing around and past us, we are reminded that we participate in the flow of God's abundant goodness. And we need reminding because sometimes we lose this awareness. Sometimes we block the flow. We receive much and don't release; or we release, pouring out, but don't receive and replenish. As we prepare for Sabbath, before we immerse our bodies in this river, I invite you to consider what in your life you need to release, and in its place, what you need to receive."

A man to my far left bellowed into the mountain air, "I release anger, and I receive calm." Then the man to his right followed, "I release unforgiveness and receive freedom." The releasing and receiving confessions channeled upstream through several men until the lot fell to me.

The tinkling sound of flowing water amplified the silence as I rummaged nervously through the hull of my heart, seeking something to say. I knew what I wanted to receive, that much was clear to me—trust.

However, the word to convey what I wanted to release, this sense of angst and tension and internal heaviness, was more elusive.

I could feel the word buried in the question that weighed me down in the water: *Will I have enough?*

Will I have enough money? Enough time? Enough of whatever it takes to stand firm in the current of unrelenting threats to my security?

I didn't want to feel this way. I wanted to feel confident and calm and at ease. I wanted to live with open hands, rather than white-knuckling my way through life. But for so long, I'd attempted to satisfy this deeply human need for security in unhealthy ways. My instincts, forged in fear, had become weapons that my own mind used against my well-being.

*Release striving and receive trust.*

Slowly, the word for what I desired to release bubbled to the surface. And in that moment, while I wanted to unleash my releasing-and-receiving cry like the man to my far left, I couldn't. My heart was bound up in my throat.

"Striving," I whispered. "I release striving and receive trust."

After fasting forty days and forty nights, he was hungry. And the tempter came and said to him, "[Since] you are the Son of God, command these stones to become loaves of bread." But he answered, "It is written,

> "'Man shall not live by bread alone,
>     but by every word that comes from the mouth
>         of God.'"[1]

Most of Jesus' childhood is hidden in history, shrouded in speculation. We know the drama that surrounded his birth,[2] and we catch a glimpse of him as a prodigious twelve-year-old sitting in the Temple.[3] But aside from this, the Scriptures are virtually silent, which isn't unusual. In his era, stories of important figures often didn't chronicle childhood years—unless, that is, there was something truly exceptional about that person's upbringing.[4] The silence speaks for itself—Jesus' early years probably weren't anything to write home about. Or at least, not anything to write Gospels about.

As far as we know—and we can't know for certain—Jesus had a normal upbringing living in a blue-collar Jewish family. He likely apprenticed with Joseph in the family trade, spending untold hours milling his way around a workshop. Authors Leonard Sweet and Frank Viola imagine what it may have been like:

> He would perspire. He would toil. He would get
> His clothes dirty. He would become exhausted. He
> would learn the physical labor of cutting wood,
> mixing mortar, hauling stone, and working with

a mallet, ax, and trowel. He would know the agonies of labor as well as its joys. Just like most of us.[5]

When Jesus worked, he didn't multiply lumber or finish a project with the snap of his fingers. He put in the hours; he showed up when he'd rather have stayed home.

As we gaze into the fog of his adolescence, poking our heads through the old wooden door of a lantern-lit workshop, we can see that Jesus' early years weren't lost—they just probably weren't lustrous. They were, however, preparing him for the responsibilities that would be thrust on him.

After Mary and Joseph took Jesus to the Temple at age twelve, we don't see Joseph again in the pages of Scripture. This is most likely because he died sometime after this moment, making Jesus the man of the house, as he was the eldest son. Now all those years of apprenticeship would prove handy as Jesus quite possibly shouldered the load of providing for his family—his mother, four brothers, and sisters. As a primary breadwinner, Jesus would have known what any laborer knew: It only takes a good run of bad luck, bad weather, or bad customers to leave you wishing you had the power to multiply a meal.[6]

Or to turn stones to bread.

As Jesus faced his first temptation, he may have had in mind the many mouths he could feed, the pain and suffering he could alleviate by turning stones to bread. And with the devil's words pointing back to the Exodus, Jesus certainly had in mind the many mouths that his Father fed when he led his people out of Egypt.

✦

God had extracted Israel from 430 years of Egyptian slavery,[7] pummeling their oppressors with cosmic plagues—a well-earned retribution, in Israelite minds. Pharaoh, ruler of Egypt, shuddered at the thought of losing his workforce, so he mounted his chariot and summoned his men to pursue the fleeing Israelites, cornering them at the Red Sea.

But God caused a strong east wind to blow, parting the water into walls on either side of his people, who scampered across the seafloor to safety. Then the walls collapsed, burying the Egyptians.

Israel belted a "Hallelujah" chorus. Faith in God reached fever pitch.

Then tides turned. Israel entered wilderness . . . and food supplies soon disappeared.

Physical hunger pangs fueled distrust and resentment as the people set crosshairs on Moses. "Would that we had died by the hand of the LORD in the land of Egypt," they complained, "when we sat by the meat pots and ate bread to the full, for you have brought us out into this wilderness to kill this whole assembly with hunger."[8]

God intervened by causing manna to fall from the sky. Through Moses, the Lord instructed the people to gather enough each morning for their family to eat that day—a test of whether they would walk in his commands. Some failed the test by keeping manna overnight, and in the morning it rotted. On the sixth day, the instructions changed. On this day, twice as much as usual should be gathered and prepared, and the extra would not rot overnight. On the seventh day, the Sabbath, they'd eat leftovers and should gather no bread. Again, many failed the test, seeking to gather instead of resting on the Sabbath, focusing on the bread and not God's words about the bread.

With this bread-from-heaven rhythm, God was training Israel to trust him as their source of security, to obey his commands, and to put their confidence in every word that proceeded from his mouth.[9]

> God was training Israel to trust him as their source of security, to obey his commands, and to put their confidence in every word that proceeded from his mouth.

This story from Exodus 16 was why, in the Jewish (and later, Christian) mind, bread became a symbol: God provides for us now as God provided for Israel in the wilderness.

With this understanding of the significance of bread, we can see that the temptation to turn stones to bread wasn't just an invitation for Jesus to assuage his hunger but rather to provide for himself—and eventually, the masses who would follow him—apart from trusting in God.

You may recall that Jesus turned water to wine, and after that multiplied bread and fish as food for thousands.[10] These works of his were celebrated in the Gospels as miracles, as the power of God on display. We might ask, *Why is it unacceptable during Jesus' first temptation to turn stones to bread yet acceptable to turn water to wine and multiply food supplies later?*

It all comes down to what the rabbis call *kavanah*, which means "intention."

I was once lamenting to my rabbi friend Arthur Kurzweil about a situation at work. A colleague had created a host of challenges that I now had to unravel. I bellyached about my colleague's arrogance, lack of thoughtfulness, and sheer stupidity.

Arthur patiently listened, and when I stopped ranting, allowed a pause. Then he relayed a story that's helped me in countless situations since.

"Let's say that you're driving down the road, and someone cuts you off in traffic," he began. "And you're already late for work, and he causes you to get stuck at a long red light. You're probably fuming, right? You're shocked at how inconsiderate he is. You pound on the steering wheel and shout at him as he speeds into the distance."

"I could imagine myself doing something like that," I replied.

Arthur continued, "Now let's say that instead of assuming that the driver is inconsiderate, you know he's just learned that his child was badly injured at school, and he's rushing to the hospital. How do you feel now?"

I responded, "I suppose that I would breathe a prayer for him and his child, and I would hope that he got there quickly and that the child would be okay."

Arthur ended the lesson: "You get to decide how you perceive people's intentions."

The rabbi was helping me understand the power of *kavanah*, intention. Assuming that my coworker's intention was to make my work more cumbersome, or that he was acting out of negligence or lack of care, would foster anger and resentment and lead me to distance myself from him.

However, if I assumed that perhaps he was distracted because he might be experiencing hardship at home, or perhaps while he genuinely desired to do good work that would benefit the team, he simply overlooked some details that created problems with the project—I would have a different outlook on the situation and a healthier disposition toward him. Then I might reach out to him for a conversation about how we could work better together, rather than cold-shouldering and working around him.

One perspective leads to alienation; the other to reconciliation.

Certainly, we should not push this wisdom to its extreme ends and naively suffer at another's hands, accepting their harmful actions by justifying their potentially noble intentions. But we should acknowledge that we're often far too quick to assume the worst of intentions in others.

Intentions matter, and they matter deeply before the Lord, who looks not on the outside but at the heart.[11]

If we look at the Temptation through the lens of *kavanah*, we catch a glimpse of the reason Jesus resisted turning stones to bread. His desire was to do the will of his Father, not to strive in his own power to meet his needs. Like a surfer looking for a wave that the ocean created, Jesus moved in the direction of his Father's activity, only doing what he saw his Father doing, accepting only the invitations that his Father gave him.[12] Everything Jesus did flowed from this relationship with his Father.

> *Everything Jesus did flowed from this relationship with his Father.*

"What's he doing?" I asked my friends as we reclined on the beach. In the distance, a man sprinted along the shoreline, his left arm outstretched beside him as an indiscernible object trailed behind some ten yards.

As he drew near, it became apparent that he was trying to fly a kite. The only problem was there was absolutely no wind, so his efforts to keep the kite in the air were contingent on how swift he could run. For a brief stretch, he'd dash as fast as he could, and the kite would sail. When he'd run out of energy, the kite would plummet. Then he'd stop, catch his breath, and begin running again.

By now, he'd attracted a small audience of beachgoers. They cheered as his kite intermittently rose to as high as twenty feet in the air. When he rested as he lost energy, they lost interest. He repeated his futile attempts as he sprinted down the shoreline and dissolved into the horizon.

*It's tough to fly a kite when there is no wind*, I thought. And the next thought was no less obvious but all the more piercing: *That's how so much of my life feels—like I'm trying to fly a kite without wind.*

For a kite to really soar, you need wind. You need an outside force to hoist the kite into the sky. You certainly have a role to play in flying the kite; but you realize that your role is limited, and your own efforts will take you only so far. Your role is to wait for the wind. You hold the string and pay attention to the direction you need to head. But all the while, even while you're running around, you understand that you're not really the one flying the kite. The wind flies the kite.

This moment happened toward the beginning of my ministry some two decades ago, and it still makes me think of the times when I've strived to produce results in my own power. How, when I thought things might fly off the rails or when I was afraid for my security, I pushed ahead of God's pace to achieve the results I wanted, rather than waiting on God to act and getting in on his activity. I think of how wearied I often felt.

It pains me to consider how much energy I burned, how much peace I forsook. How I grinded it out at work, not because I was up against a deadline but because I so often felt that my back was up against a wall and my security was in peril. It grieves me to consider the many years I acted out of fear and manipulated people and situations to my advantage so that I would be viewed favorably by my superiors. I lament how results-focused I was, while losing sight of things that truly matter in life.

I missed out on so many moments of joy and peace because I was bent on making something happen, one way or another. Deep down, I didn't trust God. I was afraid that God would not give me what I needed when I needed it, that God could not be taken at his word. I was afraid that God did not really have good intentions toward me.

And it was this underlying fear, this fundamental distrust, that motivated so much of my striving for security for so many years. And while I wish I could retrace my steps and undo my past, those missed moments have washed away like that kite runner's footprints in the sand.

And maybe that's why, when I stepped into that river in the summer of 2014, as a cool breeze brushed across my neck, my aching heart caught in my throat. I could only utter the faintest of prayers: "I release striving and receive trust."

Those many years of striving had carved deep contours through the landscape of my soul that I knew I couldn't repair in a moment of inspiration by shouting at the sky. No, I'd have to trust that a simple whisper in the ears of my Father would be enough to begin the healing process.

✦ ✦

As I left the retreat center and boarded the train to the airport to head home, I contemplated that beautiful and awkward moment in the river—the shock to my senses as I entered the cool, rushing water; the solidarity that reverberated through the atmosphere as men released and received things most intimate and true; the hope that I would find some peace and learn to trust.

I thought about how, when we'd all released and received, we fell headlong into the river, and how refreshed I felt. And about how my heart felt a little lighter as we walked back through the field to the truck.

And as our plane circled New York City and I peered through my window at the tiny tops of buildings that minutes earlier had towered overhead, my problems seemed a little smaller—and the days ahead felt a little less foreboding.

I had miles to go before I would arrive home; a long journey awaited. And on that long flight back, I sensed that I had many more miles to go before I'd learn how to move from striving to trust. This was only the beginning of a journey toward learning to see the world in a new way. But I also sensed an invitation. Somewhere ahead there was a better way, a different mindset, that would help me settle this question in my soul: *Will I have enough?*

# INVITATION:
# CHOOSE TO TRUST

I HARDLY DREAM, AND WHEN I DO, I rarely remember the dream when I awaken. But one night, I dreamed a dream that escaped the bonds of sleep.

A couple of weeks prior, my wife, Elizabeth, had told me she was pregnant, which was a delight to us both, as for many months we'd sought to conceive another child. We broadly shared the news.

Because the first pregnancy had progressed normally, we had no concerns about the second. And for the first few weeks, we had no reason to worry. Until I dreamed my dream.

In the dream, Elizabeth and I walked into an OB-GYN clinic. I didn't recognize this clinic; the one we visited during her first pregnancy was in another state. We went through the usual protocol—paperwork, sitting in a lobby awaiting our appointment, thumbing through magazines, and so on.

When Elizabeth's name was called, we walked down a hallway. A technician weighed her, measured her height, and then guided us into the room for examination.

I can still remember the contents of the room as vividly today as when I saw them in my dream. There were two blue chairs along one wall, a bathroom behind my left shoulder, and an examination table directly in front of me—head end of the table to my left, stirrups to the right.

Elizabeth sat on the table as we made small talk and waited. Eventually, a nurse, who appeared to be of Asian descent, entered the room, examined Elizabeth, and said, looking at her and then at me, "I'm so sorry."

I awakened from the dream in a cold sweat.

I didn't want to alarm Elizabeth, so I didn't share the dream with her. I reasoned that it was just a dream. But it didn't feel like just a dream. I journaled about the dream, and later that day I sat with my senior pastor in his office and shared the dream with him.

"When is your doctor's visit?" he asked.

"Maybe in a couple of weeks. I'm not sure," I responded.

"I think you should go with her," he said.

I had no intention of missing the appointment.

I still didn't share my dream with Elizabeth. I saw no benefit in creating any concern in her mind. But when she informed me that she was spotting blood, I inquired as to the date of the doctor's visit. Thankfully, it was soon.

When the day for the appointment arrived and we entered the clinic, everything appeared as one would expect—rows of chairs lining walls, televisions projecting news and talk shows, old magazines. We checked in and awaited our appointment.

It wasn't until Elizabeth's name was called and we entered the hallway that I realized I'd been in the building before—in my dream.

The technician guided Elizabeth to the scale and took her measurements and then led us to the examination room. Everything was situated precisely as in the dream—two blue chairs, bathroom behind my left shoulder, exam table in front of me.

When an Asian nurse entered the room, my heart sank, and my legs felt numb. She examined Elizabeth and said to us, "I'm so sorry." My worst dream was realized.

The nurse left the room. We sat in silence, then tears, then anger, disbelief, and a rush of other emotions that flooded our hearts.

We'd prayed for this baby. The unborn child had already taken on a life of its own in our imagination. We'd begun decorating the room and thinking of names, and we had told little Seri that she would become a big sister. It was devastating to have such a dream dashed in a matter of moments.

And it's even more unnerving when you've dreamed a dream that foretells your greatest fear, which then becomes reality.

We held the news close for a while but soon informed family and friends of our loss. Most troubling of all were conversations with churchgoers, who, when they heard the news, offered well-meaning but ill-advised condolences.

"God needed another flower in his garden," some would say.

"God needed another angel in the choir," comforted others.

At first, I'd just nod and walk away, understanding that they were seeking to help. But over time, I grew impatient with their platitudes.

"If God needs flowers, someone up there should plant them," I'd snap. "And if angels are needed in the choir, some-one should recruit. Unborn babies do not become flowers or angels."

As time passed, their condolences waned. Our grieving, however, was just beginning. And while the grieving process was not easy for Elizabeth, she found the grace to process the miscarriage in as healthy a way as possible.

The process for me, however, was very different. I was the one who'd had the dream. Why would God give me a dream foreshadowing the whole order of events? And why would God create a baby in my wife's womb only to allow her or him to die seven weeks into the pregnancy?

My trust in God was shaken.

In the first temptation we clamor for a sense of security and seek to answer the question, *Will I have enough?* It's another way of asking, *Am I*

> Will I have enough? *is another way of asking,* Am I safe?

*safe?* This question is foundational to our existence. Before we can live with confidence and peace, we need to know the answer.

For most of my life, trust came easy to me. Likely as a result of being raised in a small town and a stable home environment with caring parents, I don't recall having difficulty trusting God (or other people, for that matter). And for most of my childhood and even into early adulthood, I wasn't the type of person who worried overly much.

But something happened to me during the miscarriage experience that I'm still seeking to understand. When my trust in God was shaken, the tremors of insecurity reverberated into other areas of my life for many years. And though they've dissipated over time, I still feel the aftershocks when I least expect them.

I've longed for the simplicity of heart and mind that I had in my childhood. But naivete can't stand in the face of adversity and won't undo the deep wounds that life inflicts. Something stronger is needed, something forged in the fires of suffering that does not destroy trust but deepens it.

Despite pain, doubt, and despair, embers of hope remained—and I found a way forward through the temptations of Christ. Let's allow him to guide us into a deeper sense of trusting God, so we can live with a sense of security that transcends our circumstances. Let's allow his mindset to become ours.

+

After Jesus' wilderness temptations, word of his miracles spread rapidly—and large crowds followed. On one such occasion, some five thousand men, and even more women and children with them, gathered as he sat on a mountainside.

Noticing the rising tide of humanity, Jesus turned to his disciple Philip and asked, "Where are we to buy bread, so that these people may eat?" Philip estimated that six months of earnings wouldn't be enough to provide each person with even a little bread.

Another disciple, Andrew, remarked, "There is a boy here who has five barley loaves and two fish, but what are they for so many?" The answer was as obvious to him as it was to everyone around him—not enough.

Despite having seen Jesus turn water to wine, not one of his disciples thought that the answer to Jesus' question was in fact the person asking the question.

But Jesus knew what he would do even before he asked Philip the question, for he said this to test him. And to their astonishment, Jesus took the bread and fish, gave thanks to God, multiplied them, and commanded the disciples to collect the leftovers after everyone had their fill.

Following the miracle, Jesus withdrew again to the

mountain by himself, for he perceived that they sought to force him to become king. As evening came, his disciples set sail for Capernaum. In the pitch of night, Jesus came to them, walking on water, and boarded their boat as a storm buffeted the vessel. They safely arrived ashore, where the crowds joined them the following day.[1]

Sometimes God intervenes.

Sometimes God withdraws.

Sometimes those are one and the same.

For years, I couldn't speak about our miscarriage. I couldn't find any answers to settle the gnawing, soul-scathing, honest-to-God questions that plagued my mind. Why did God allow this to happen? Did I do something to deserve this? Did I not do something that I should have done? Was God teaching me a lesson? Did I not have enough faith or pray diligently enough, in the shadow of the dream, to forestall a calamity about which God had warned me?

*Sometimes God intervenes.*
*Sometimes God withdraws.*
*Sometimes those are*
*one and the same.*

And then there was the problem of what I'll call my idea of a good and loving "omni-God": that God is omnipresent (all-present); omniscient (all-knowing); and omnipotent (all-powerful). Despite my best efforts, I couldn't reconcile how God—who created the baby in its womb-become-grave—could have foreseen and stopped the miscarriage but did not. *If God were a truly loving God,* I thought, *he was either not present, not aware, or not capable.*

I sought God in every logical corner of my mind and in all my doctrines and dogmas and tried-and-true beliefs, but he was nowhere to be found. God was hidden.

And with the sense of God's absence increasing, my sense of security decreased. If this could happen to me, what else lurked around the corner? If God could not be trusted to manage this matter to my satisfaction, how else would God disappoint?

I'd long believed in a God who could multiply loaves and fish to feed thousands, but I couldn't comprehend a God who would not meet me at this point of need. I grew to understand why Philip said to Jesus, "Two hundred denarii worth of bread would not be enough for each of them to get a little." I empathized with Andrew: "There is a boy here who has five barley loaves and two fish, but what are they for so many?"

I came to perceive the world as a place of lack, a place where there's not enough to meet the demands and difficulties that come my way. The world is filled with problems—was for them, is for us. For every person Jesus cured, he simply passed by another. For every mouth Jesus fed, thousands more gaped for bread. More times than not, in the face of adversity, we just don't have what it takes and often don't get what we want.

Life is difficult and full of trouble.

I slowly lost the simplehearted, openhanded trust of a little boy who could offer the load he carried to Jesus, and my burden became too much to bear. I forsook the belief that God would meet my needs.

Like the crowd who was surely disappointed when the Jesus they wanted to become their king withdrew to the mountain by himself, I couldn't find God to save my life.

✠

When they found him on the other side of the sea, they said to him, "Rabbi, when did you come here?" Jesus answered them, "Truly, truly, I say to you, you are seeking me, not because you saw signs, but because you ate your fill of the loaves. Do not work for the food that perishes, but for the food that endures to eternal life, which the Son of Man will give to you. For on him God the Father has set his seal." Then they said to him, "What must we do, to be doing the works of God?" Jesus answered them, "This is the work of God, that you believe in him whom he has sent." So they said to him, "Then what sign do you do, that we may see and believe you? What work do you perform? Our fathers ate the manna in the wilderness; as it is written, 'He gave them bread from heaven to eat.'" Jesus then said to them, "Truly, truly, I say to you, it was not Moses who gave you the bread from heaven, but my Father gives you the true bread from heaven. For the bread

of God is he who comes down from heaven and
gives life to the world." They said to him, "Sir, give
us this bread always."

Jesus said to them, "I am the bread of life;
whoever comes to me shall not hunger, and whoever
believes in me shall never thirst."

"Truly, truly, I say to you, unless you eat the flesh
of the Son of Man and drink his blood, you have no
life in you. Whoever feeds on my flesh and drinks
my blood has eternal life, and I will raise him up on
the last day. For my flesh is true food, and my blood
is true drink. Whoever feeds on my flesh and drinks
my blood abides in me, and I in him. As the living
Father sent me, and I live because of the Father,
so whoever feeds on me, he also will live because
of me."[2]

Jesus really needed a PR person. Just when he was beginning to draw crowds, just when his ministry was really gaining momentum, he started telling people to eat his flesh and
drink his blood. You'll have to forego the temptation to sym-
bolize flesh and blood as the Eucharist here for a moment
because while all that is certainly in play symbolically, that's
not how it literally played out in the minds of his hearers. To
them, Jesus was out of his mind.

At this point, even many of his disciples left him.
Honestly, who could blame them? But for some reason, some

remained, and Jesus asked them, "Do you want to go away as well?" Peter responded on behalf of the Twelve: "Lord, to whom shall we go? You have the words of eternal life, and we have believed, and have come to know, that you are the Holy One of God."[3]

What Peter says is just as astonishing to me as what he doesn't say. He doesn't say that they're staying because they saw him turn water to wine. He doesn't say that it's because he healed the sick or fed thousands with spartan supplies that they're still hanging around. He says that there's something about his words that won't let them leave.

Jesus' words were true, deep, transformational, and life-giving. They were hanging and banking on every word that came from his mouth.

At the time, I didn't have language to describe my experience of God's absence, which lasted off and on for years. I was unaware that over the centuries the saints have described this sensation as a "dark night of the soul."[4] And I had no way of knowing that in this perceived absence, God was trusting me to seek him through the darkness.

But one afternoon during that painful season, as I was reading a book in my study, I stumbled upon a line written by Julian of Norwich: "All shall be well, and all shall be well, and all manner of thing shall be well."[5]

I was arrested by those simple words: *All shall be well.*

I read them over and over again. And as I read them, those painful memories surfaced: the dream, the death, the doubts, the anxieties, the questions for God.

And for reasons I cannot explain, even as my questions remained, the presence of God settled something inside my soul in that moment that no rational explanation of the problem of suffering could resolve.

All wasn't well in that moment, but somehow I became open to the possibility that all *shall* be well. That despite my lingering questions, God was not offended by them and shunning me but was nearer to me than I knew. My questions, as I lived them and deeply wrestled with them, carried me back toward a place of trusting God.

While it would take a book unto itself to lead you through every twist and turn of this journey back to trust, I slowly realized that it was the categories into which I'd put God that needed to change, not God's intentions or actions toward me.

In my charmed existence, I'd come to believe that it was God's job to protect me from harm and to give me what I wanted. And, like Jesus withdrawing from the crowd who would crown him king, God refused to meet my expectations. In my suffering, I came to understand that sometimes we experience God's power through his protection, but in a broken world, sometimes we experience God's power through his consolation. As we weep, God weeps too.

Sometimes God saves the day. Sometimes God says with the nurse, "I'm so sorry," and begins the healing process. But all the time and in all things, God works for the good of those who love him and are "called according to his purpose."[6]

And while I cannot claim that God caused the pain, I will stake my life on the reality that amid the pain, God caused me to trust him in ways I never would have had I not experienced that pain.

✦

I'll never understand everything Jesus had in mind when he shocked the crowd by telling them that they had to eat his flesh and drink his blood. I'm unsure, had I been numbered among them, whether I would have remained or left. His words were too deep for most people to comprehend back then, and they're surely too deep for me to fully digest today.

But I think his words about being the Bread of Life, about eating his flesh and drinking his blood, have something to do with taking him in—his words and actions and entire essence—and letting him fill your heart and mind and whole being.

I think it means that we can't separate Jesus' words and actions from who he is—it's all one. Jesus is what Jesus says and does, so to receive his words and take them to heart is to receive him and take him in.

I think it has something to do with not placing your security in your own resources—whether that's a bank account, retirement savings, or even just the next paycheck—but rather in the Living Bread, who feeds your soul in ways that truly satisfy.

I think it has something to do with believing that, come

what may, though we run out of bread and find our flesh and blood spilled on the earth's altar, God has the power to raise the dead on the last day.

And it's for this reason that, when Jesus talks about being Living Bread and us eating his flesh and drinking his blood, I think he's talking about trust. He's talking about not living by bread alone but by banking your entire life, all your hopes and dreams and your full sense of security, on every word that comes from the mouth of God.

He's saying that everything he did and said was out of a tight-knit relationship with his living Father. His Father was as real to him as his right arm. Jesus knew his Father was as close as the air he breathed.[7] And he was clear in his desires for you and me to enter relationship with him as he'd entered relationship with his Father, to feast on him as he'd feasted on his Father's every word.[8]

And that's the essence of trust—not that we project expectations onto a relationship, demanding we always get what we want; but that we receive, believe, and obey every word that comes from the mouth of God because we take God at his word. Trust is believing that these words from this same God who commanded manna to fall from the sky can satisfy our truest needs.

The manna story, after all, was never about a meal. No, it was always about trust. As Moses put it:

He humbled you and let you hunger and fed you
with manna, which you did not know, nor did

your fathers know, that he might make you know that man does not live by bread alone, but man lives by every word that comes from the mouth of the LORD.[9]

And so, rather than turning stones to bread, Jesus places his full trust in his Father and lives not by striving but by every word that comes from the mouth of God.

At his word, all striving ceases. At his word, all storms are stilled. At his word, your soul is satisfied and your deepest needs are met. At his word, at the end of days, you shall rise. And if the final hour belongs to God, you need not fear the next second.[10]

*Trust is believing that these words from this same God who commanded manna to fall from the sky can satisfy our truest needs.*

The temptation to strive is only a temporary and illusory shortcut to meet our need for security. Only in the mindset of trust do we find the pathway to resist striving. But how do we cultivate this mindset? For that, we must do the opposite of strive.

We must rest.

# PRACTICE:
# REST IN SABBATH

"COVER YOUR EYES," SAID OUR HOST, motioning gently to the guests who'd gathered at the table at one of the Jewish retreat center's cabins. "Sabbath is the queen of days, and we welcome it with reverence."

She struck a match and prayed as the faint scent of smoke wafted by. Her soft words were bathed in serenity and dignity. "Open your eyes," she invited. "Sabbath has arrived." The amber hue of a candle's glow illumined our faces; smiles crept ear to ear.

I'd rarely experienced such calm, a fitting end to the day I'd spent at the river. That week, and that day, lingers still. It seems like a month's worth of living was packed into that brief visit. Perhaps that's because of the idyllic conversations by lakes, mountain lookouts, and waterfalls. Or maybe it's because we abandoned our tech devices and paid attention to the land, to Scripture, and to one another.

Whatever the cause, the seeds planted that week germinated in my mind and have grown into fond memories over the years.

There was something holy about that space—and not just the place but the pace.

+

The morning after my first Sabbath meal around that farm-style table, I inquired of one of the rabbis, "In order to keep the Sabbath with my wife and children, what do we need to stop doing? Like, we're not Jewish, but I can tell there's something special about the Sabbath experience."

He replied, "Everyone thinks that Sabbath is about what they must stop doing, and to some extent, it is. But for starters, for a family like yours, begin doing one thing that you all never get to do that brings joy, and pay attention to what happens."

> *"Begin doing one thing that you all never get to do that brings joy, and pay attention to what happens."*
> —A WISE RABBI

I was expecting a litany of *thou shalt nots* and instead received encouragement to do something we loved. This was my brand of rabbi.

His admonition rattled in my brain in the weeks following.

One evening during dinner with my family, I asked, "What's one fun thing that we never get to do that we could do on Sabbath?" I'd failed to discern that my crew had hardly any concept of what Sabbath was, so I had to lay a bit of biblical groundwork. Once I did, our two children fired away with ideas ranging from going to Disney World every week to riding a spotted unicorn who poops Skittles. Apparently, I portrayed my Sabbath experience with such enthusiasm that they thought anything was possible.

They eventually started thinking more realistically. "Let's eat outside on Sabbath," proposed one. "Yeah, that's awesome. Let's eat outside every Sabbath," affirmed the other. Getting two children who are five years apart in age to agree on any proposed activity is an act of God, so we rolled with it.

Our first Sabbath table was set at lunchtime in our garden. Paper plates, plump with macaroni and cheese and not-even-close-to-kosher hot dogs, littered our rickety picnic table. It was time for the blessing.

Not knowing any special Sabbath prayers, I recalled the moment in the river when my friends and I practiced releasing and receiving. So I asked each member of our family to consider one thing they would like to release and one thing they'd like to receive.

I began, releasing striving and receiving trust. Elizabeth released frustration and received patience. Our then-preteen daughter, Seri, released talking back and received respect; and finally, our younger child, Seth, had his moment.

"I release candy!" he exclaimed with such zeal that I thought he'd confused the definitions of *releasing* and *receiving*. Then he brought things full circle: "I release candy, and I receive presents! Lots of presents!" We roared with laughter; Seth seemed satisfied.

A picnic table meal in early afternoon progressed into backyard soccer, catch, walking in the garden, and otherwise loafing around.

We'd found our one thing, and this one thing continued to evolve Sabbath after Sabbath. Easy-to-cook meals prepped indoors and eaten outside morphed into open-flame grilling over our firepit. Our children began inviting their friends, who invited their parents, to cook over the fire. The simplicity was intoxicating.

The same sense of losing track of time that engulfed me at the retreat occurred during those Sabbath suppers in our own backyard. The same delight that I saw in faces around that farm-style table shone through the wide-eyed smiles of my own children as our campfire cast its glow on them.

And as I took it all in, week after week during that first summer of fumbling around with Sabbath keeping, I began to feel the sense of heaviness I'd carried with me for years slowly lighten. The incessant churn of my mind settled, if only for a day.

I thought Sabbath was all about the work I could not do, but Sabbath was in fact doing deep work on me.

Then the LORD said to Moses, "Behold, I am about
to rain bread from heaven for you, and the people
shall go out and gather a day's portion every day, that
I may test them, whether they will walk in my law
or not. On the sixth day, when they prepare what
they bring in, it will be twice as much as they gather
daily." . . .

And the people of Israel did so. They gathered,
some more, some less. But when they measured it
with an omer, whoever gathered much had nothing
left over, and whoever gathered little had no lack.
Each of them gathered as much as he could eat.
And Moses said to them, "Let no one leave any of
it over till the morning." But they did not listen to
Moses. Some left part of it till the morning, and it
bred worms and stank. And Moses was angry with
them. Morning by morning they gathered it, each
as much as he could eat; but when the sun grew hot,
it melted.

On the sixth day they gathered twice as much
bread, two omers each. And when all the leaders
of the congregation came and told Moses, he said
to them, "This is what the LORD has commanded:
'Tomorrow is a day of solemn rest, a holy Sabbath
to the LORD; bake what you will bake and boil what
you will boil, and all that is left over lay aside to be
kept till the morning.'" So they laid it aside till the
morning, as Moses commanded them, and it did not

stink, and there were no worms in it. Moses said, "Eat it today, for today is a Sabbath to the LORD; today you will not find it in the field. Six days you shall gather it, but on the seventh day, which is a Sabbath, there will be none."

On the seventh day some of the people went out to gather, but they found none. And the LORD said to Moses, "How long will you refuse to keep my commandments and my laws? See! The LORD has given you the Sabbath; therefore on the sixth day he gives you bread for two days. Remain each of you in his place; let no one go out of his place on the seventh day." So the people rested on the seventh day.[1]

Complexity wasn't the problem. The instructions were simple. Five days a week, God's people would demonstrate their obedience and trust in God's word by gathering only enough manna for that day. Only on the sixth day were they to gather twice as much. On the seventh day, they demonstrated their trust in God not by working to gather manna but by *not* working—by resting and enjoying what God had already provided.

Sometimes trust calls for action; sometimes trust calls for rest. Trusting God in our rest is often just as difficult—if not more so—than trusting God in our work. At least when we work, we feel some sense of control over our lives. But in rest, we're releasing control. As the Israelites demonstrate, this is an ongoing challenge of the human condition: We're inclined to strive, to make something happen, to push ourselves beyond healthy limits to answer the question, *Will I have enough?*

A mindset of trust in God buffers us against the temptation to strive. But how do we develop this mindset? Where does this deep trust—the same that emboldened Jesus to respond to the tempter with the words of God—come from? We need more than theory; we need practicable ways to strengthen our souls to trust.

> *Trusting God in our rest is often just as difficult—if not more so—than trusting God in our work.*

Sabbath is just such a way. Author Lynne Baab writes,

> We are drawn to the words of Jesus about abundant life and his peace that passes understanding, but often we don't know how to access them. The sabbath is a concrete way to start, a practical and ancient solution to an enduring human need.[2]

Throughout the centuries, volumes have been written on the topic of Sabbath, so I won't attempt to cover everything in brief that others have probed in depth. Rather, we're going to explore Sabbath keeping together so that you can create a truly life-giving Sabbath experience for yourself and your family—and guard your heart and mind against the temptation to strive for security.

In my early days of ministry, I led a worship band composed of teenagers. Our vocalists were strong, and most of our instrumentalists were fairly competent. We had only one problem—the drummer. A drummer's job is to set and keep the beat, but our drummer didn't do that. Instead, he'd adapt his rhythm to another musician's rhythm.

I tried to help him. More than once in practice, I turned to him and said, "I know you're trying hard, but your job is to keep the rhythm; our job is to follow you as you follow it." Instead, despite his best efforts and my futile attempts to assist, he usually ended up following someone else's rhythm.

It was a mess. Once the band lost the beat, it was nearly impossible for us to find it again. We couldn't tweak our way back into rhythm because we all ended up just chasing one another rhythmically. Sometimes the only thing we could do was stop the song and start over.

When I think about Sabbath, I think about rhythm. And when I think about rhythm, I think about how sometimes the best way to find the right rhythm is to call for a full stop.

And pause.

And rest.

There's an ancient, primal rhythm that pulsates through the deepest part of who I am, of who you are. The rhythm can be tough to hear, buried beneath the noise of life. But it's there. It always has been. The Genesis poem helps us hear this rhythm.

Thus the heavens and the earth were finished, and all the host of them. And on the seventh day God finished his work that he had done, and he rested on the seventh day from all his work that he had done. So God blessed the seventh day and made it holy, because on it God rested from all his work that he had done in creation.[3]

Six days of work, one day of rest—God's six-one rhythm for creating and the created order. This rhythm is woven into the fabric of reality, threading its way through time and the cosmos. We are born into this rhythm, and we are beckoned to dance the dance of our lives within it.

But it's easy to lose the beat, and when we do, we feel it. Maybe our work lacks meaning. Maybe we lose creativity. Maybe our interest in relationships fizzles. Maybe our stress levels ping the limit, and we feel always on edge. Maybe we don't have words for the way that we feel off, out of sync. And maybe there are many reasons for this. But one of them could be because we've lost the rhythm for which we were created.

When we lose the six-one rhythm of creation, one day bleeds into the next. Before we realize it, as the Jewish Sabbath prayer makes plain, "Days pass and the years vanish, and we walk sightless among miracles."[4] Our lives lose their harmony; our identity becomes muddled and wrapped up too tightly in what we do and what we create. Eventually, we can't distinguish ourselves from our work. People ask us who we are, and we tell them what we do for a living.

The creation narrative in Genesis offers us a better way. Genesis 1:1 is often translated, "In the beginning, God created . . ." Now, it's not that this translation is wrong, but there are other ways to render this verse. Some Hebrew scholars translate these words with a nuance that is quite interesting: "When God began to create . . ."[5]

In the first case—"In the beginning, God created"—we may come away believing that the first thing we should understand about God is that he makes things. In the second, we are invited to consider that the beginning of God and the beginning of God's creative work are not one and the same.

*When God began to create* helps us realize that God existed before God created—an obvious statement with profound implications. Before God creates, God is.

The story later teaches us that humans are created in the image of God.[6] So if before God creates, God is, then as divine image bearers, we are more than what we make. Like God, we are not what we create, earn, or produce. This realization contradicts a culture that binds our identity to our accomplishments.

*A better rhythm, a healthier way to move through life, begins with the realization that we are not what we create.*

While we might nod our heads in agreement—of course we are more than what we create—our behavior often indicates that this understanding hasn't made the eighteen-inch journey from the head to the heart. Take away what we do, and we wrestle with who we are.

A better rhythm, a healthier way to move through life, begins with the realization that *we are not what we create.*

+ +

While *Sabbath* means "to stop," Sabbath is more than the absence of activity. There's a paradox in Sabbath rest, and anytime we find ourselves in a paradox—two seemingly opposing views being true about the same thing—we are usually close to wisdom.

Sabbath rest is a stop, and at the same time Sabbath rest is an activity. While you are ceasing from work, you are not doing nothing.

You are resting.

Rest is the action.

But rest doesn't come easily to many of us. We often resist rest because in our culture we so highly value productivity.

One friend of mine, a pastor, was studying the topic of Sabbath with me and a few others, wrestling with the idea that rest is something she could experience without guilt. In her childhood, she picked up the notion that rest was something lazy people did when they should have been busy working and making themselves useful. This attitude is not unusual. Much of contemporary Western culture shares this perspective about rest, achievement, and success.

But this mindset, while popular, is problematic. If rest is the enemy of productivity, and productivity is a measure of success, and success is a measure of self-worth, then Sabbath rest can threaten your identity.

As I sat with my friend and her husband, her eyes welled with tears. She shared a truth she'd been meditating on, something she had picked up from the great Rabbi Heschel. "On Sabbath, we become okay with what is. We rest as if our work is done, even if it's not."[7] She pointed out the immense power in the *as if*—it's not that there's nothing else to do; it's just that on this one day, we choose to rest *as if* there's nothing else to do.

Someone else in the group responded, "And not only can we rest *as if* there's nothing else to do, we can rest because rest is in fact the thing that we are *supposed to do*. Maybe it would help if we all added an item to our to-do list called 'Sabbath rest' and on this day we ignored everything else on the list!"

As we rest as if there's nothing else to do, we can do it without guilt. On Sabbath, rest is God's assignment for us.

+

The number-one objection I hear from Christians about practicing Sabbath is that Sabbath is an "Old Testament thing." Not only does that argument overlook the reality that Sabbath preceded the law and demonstrate a belief that Christians should just abandon the wisdom of the first two-thirds of the Bible—it also neglects to acknowledge Jesus' relationship to the Sabbath.

Jesus kept the Sabbath, and he did so not so that Christians could abandon it but to fulfill it—to return it to its proper place in people's hearts, minds, and lives. We have no record that he commanded his disciples to forsake Sabbath practice, nor do any New Testament writings command Christians to forgo Sabbath keeping.

But—and this is important—we do see Jesus seriously questioning how Sabbath was being used. In the religious context of his day, Sabbath had become a means to misery and oppression. On six occasions Jesus squared off against religious leaders regarding rules that had been added to Sabbath keeping.

However, not once did Jesus undermine the idea that the Sabbath should be kept. As Lynne Baab points out,

> Jesus' first public appearance, recorded in Luke 4, shows him reading from the scroll of Isaiah in the synagogue on the sabbath. Luke reports that it was Jesus' custom to be at the synagogue on the sabbath day.[8]

Jesus' purpose in engaging the religious leaders was to point to the purpose of Sabbath keeping and "what [it] reflects about God to the people who observe it."[9] A reading of these six Sabbath instances reveals that in five of the six occasions, the religious authorities questioned Jesus' practice of healing on the Sabbath, and in the remaining instance they questioned whether it was lawful for his disciples to satisfy their hunger by plucking grain on the Sabbath.[10] In response, Jesus persisted in healing the infirm and allowed his disciples to eat the food they picked. He viewed Sabbath as "a day to do good, show mercy, save life and free people from bondage."[11]

Jesus felt the authority to challenge the religious leaders' Sabbath views because he believed that "the Son of Man is lord of the Sabbath."[12] And the lord of the Sabbath kept the Sabbath in a way that led to human flourishing and liberation. "Acts that glorify God can never be a breach of the sabbath."[13] After all, the Sabbath was made for humans—for rest and liberation—not humans for the Sabbath.

The prophet Isaiah writes,

> If you turn back your foot from the Sabbath,
>     from doing your pleasure on my holy day,
> and call the Sabbath a delight
>     and the holy day of the LORD honorable;
> if you honor it, not going your own ways,
>     or seeking your own pleasure, or talking idly;
> then you shall take delight in the LORD,
>     and I will make you ride on the heights of the earth;
> I will feed you with the heritage of Jacob your father,
>     for the mouth of the LORD has spoken.[14]

The Sabbath is a delight when we hold it in its proper place and in the proper way, when we keep it in honor of God and love of others. When we begin with the idea that Sabbath is a delight, not a drudgery, and approach Sabbath not so much to seek what we must omit but to discern what we can include that brings rest and liberation, we're on the right track to honoring the Sabbath in a healthy way.

With these things in mind, we should never think that there is only one way we all should practice Sabbath. However, we can consider some principles and ideas that will aid us in discerning our approach to this life-giving practice:

- First, begin with the rabbi's advice: Find one thing you never get to do that brings you joy, and do that one thing on Sabbath. Get creative and decide on a Sabbath practice that you and your loved ones and friends can do together. Enjoy a special dessert or meal. Sit by a fire. Walk by a lake. Linger in a coffee shop. Whatever you do, consider how to do it with joy and ease and without pressure to get it right.

- Second, consider one thing that drains energy, and choose to *not* do it on Sabbath. This could mean that on Sabbath you do not cook a meal, vacuum your home, or check your email or social media. Whatever it is, consider one thing you will give up on Sabbath, not out of legalism but as a step toward liberty. If it feels like work, you have God's permission to figure out a way to stop doing it.

- Third, if possible, keep the Sabbath with your family or loved ones. My children look forward to Sabbath each week. Friends often join us as we pray and play, but we do our best to be together as a family and to notice the activity of God in one another. I anticipate that as our children get older, their schedules will not always align with ours on Sabbath, so we will evolve and adapt.

  You might find it best to keep the Sabbath on a day that is different from others in your closest relational circle. This is not only acceptable but also very common. I prefer to align my Sabbath as nearly as possible with the ancient tradition of sundown Friday to sundown Saturday, but your Sabbath-keeping day might even need to change over time. Go with the flow, but aim for consistency on whatever day you choose.

- Fourth, realize that what brings one person Sabbath delight might drain another. Introverts might need lots of alone time on Sabbath, while extroverts might find that a house full of friends feasting together is exactly what is needed for soul flourishing. Each person needs space—at least for part of the day—to experience rest in a way that is good for them. You might consider setting aside a few hours during Sabbath for each person to lean into what is life-giving for them.

- Finally, do your best to make your Sabbath day an actual twenty-four-hour period. Your body and mind need at least this amount of time to experience rest.

Perhaps your Sabbath will begin on Saturday evening and end on Sunday evening, likely aligning with going to church. For ministers, Sundays are days of work, so theirs might be on a Friday, Saturday, or Monday. Whatever day you pick, and whatever time of day you begin, attempt a full day's Sabbath.

However your Sabbath experience shapes up, it should promote rest and liberation, be a delight to you, and keep you centered on the Lord. Remember, Sabbath is not a day to go about business as usual. Instead, it is a gift, an opportunity to find delight and rest in God's presence and to learn to trust that God's good world can operate under his care without your intervention.

I wish I knew the name of the "do one thing you enjoy" rabbi from the retreat. I'd love to tell him how Sabbath has been a gift to my family. I'd tell him how it has brought us closer together, and I'd tell him how it has recentered us on what matters most.

But I'd also tell him how Sabbath surprised me, how I couldn't have imagined that Sabbath would speak to one of the deepest questions in my life—the question of whether I'd have enough—in such a meaningful way. I never would have dreamed that rest, not striving harder, was the solution to my enduring need for security.

His wisdom was profound. He knew that the gateway

into keeping Sabbath for someone like me was not to focus on what I needed to eliminate but to lean into things that gave me joy. These things (or in my case, this one thing) reset the rhythm of a day, and over time, the rhythm of one day reset the rhythm of my week.

Sabbath is still working on me. I still strive. I still find myself lacking trust in the Lord. I still gather when I should be resting, still white-knuckle the steering wheel of my life when I should relax my grip and enjoy the ride.

To some degree or another, I'll always wrestle with this temptation. But each week I receive an invitation to begin again, to reset, to pause and reflect on the reality that I don't live by bread alone but by every word that comes from the mouth of the One who spoke the world into existence.

Then rested.

# Am I Enough?

# TEMPTATION:
# PERFORM FOR APPROVAL

AS A PRETEEN BOY, I was allowed to wear shorts to baseball practice, but I never did. I wore sweatpants or old, stained baseball pants from a previous season.

Because we lived in northwest Florida's sweltering armpit, and because most of the other boys wore shorts to practice, people occasionally asked why I wore long pants. "Aren't you hot?" they'd inquire. "I have reasons," I assured them. "It isn't that hot to me." "I don't like sliding in shorts because I'll skin my legs." And for the most part, my logic satisfied curious minds.

But I was lying.

The reason I didn't wear pants wasn't because I didn't

want to skin my legs; I wore pants because I had skinny legs. The only change in shape from my ankles to my thighs were my knotty knees. Otherwise, it was a pencil-straight shot from floor to ceiling.

I'd been told my entire life how thin I was. I'd also been informed by my middle-school guy friends that, if by some miracle a girl was interested in physical intimacy with me, I wouldn't be able to do it, and by my baseball buddies that I wasn't big enough to fulfill my dream of becoming a professional player.

So I covered my weakness as much as possible.

One day I made a mistake. After careful examination in the mirror I observed, to my great delight, a curvature just below my knees on the back side of my legs. If I flexed hard enough, it appeared that I in fact did have what other boys took for granted—calf muscles.

I wore shorts to practice the next day, hoping someone would appreciate my recent physical development. Nobody commented, which was a good thing. Maybe I was just normal. Maybe I'd been overthinking the whole thing and my legs weren't that bad after all. I was happy to wear shorts like the other boys, and I was delighted to not be sweating my butt off.

I went to the concession stand after practice, fiddled around in my pockets for some change, and stepped up to the window to buy a soda.

"Hey, Tommy. Good practice today," remarked a teammate's father. I turned and thanked him, flexing my muscles as hard as I could, hoping that if he happened to notice my legs, he'd at least notice my calves.

"Do those hurt?" he asked.

"Does what hurt?" I replied.

He chuckled and pointed to my legs: "Those mosquito bites. Oh, wait! Those are your calf muscles."

I smiled and laughed it off.

And died inside.

And never wore shorts again to baseball practice.

Later, when I played on the basketball team, I asked for capri-length shorts, hoping to cover as much of my legs as I could. Until I was an adult, I wore pants nearly every time I played golf. I told people it was because the professionals wore pants.

But I was lying.

Even though over the years I won awards not just for athletics but also for academics, I couldn't escape the endless questions beneath all the achievement: *Am I strong enough? Tough enough? Muscular enough? Smart enough? Attractive enough? Funny enough?*

So I'd prep and primp and practice with unsurpassed diligence to ensure that the answer to all these questions was a resounding *yes*.

Yes, I made academic honor roll. Yes, I was voted *Most Likely to Succeed*. Yes, I was named *Best Dressed* in the school. Yes, to all these things and more.

And yes, I was insecure and longing for approval. Nothing quieted the questions. Nothing satisfied.

> *There is no external answer to the deeply personal question behind all my questions: Am I enough?*

Because there is no external answer to the deeply personal question behind all my questions: *Am I enough?*

To this day, the question presents itself daily. Not about my calves or strength but about my competence at work. Not about my academic prowess but about my ability to teach and preach. Not about my attractiveness but about my appeal to audiences.

The question never looks the same, but always it remains. *Am I enough?*

Then the devil took him to the holy city and set him on the pinnacle of the temple and said to him, "[Since] you are the Son of God, throw yourself down."[1]

Jesus was a small-town boy from the Galilean backwoods, his mother a poor girl impregnated by the Holy Spirit— a dubious-sounding claim that doubtless followed him his whole life—and his stepfather a simple carpenter. Jesus wasn't cut from society's finest cloth. To most, he was the kid from nowhere, the son of literally no man.

Given his beleaguered beginnings, Jesus likely never imagined that he'd stand on the Temple in the holy city, Jerusalem. The Temple was the epicenter of Jewish life, where faith, law, economics, and culture coalesced in one holy space. The Temple was also the place where Divine Presence was thought to dwell, a place of divine protection.[2] There were higher elevations, but no loftier ideal existed in Jewish minds than the Temple.

Jesus' world would have revolved around this very building for as long as he could recall. When he was young, his parents would have taken him to the holy city for festivals. Those many formative years of thrice-annual pilgrimages would have imprinted in his memory.[3] But of all his trips to Jerusalem, there was one that he'd surely never forget: the occasion his parents unwittingly left him in the Temple and began their trip home without him.[4]

Somewhere along the way, someone realized that Jesus was not numbered among the travelers. They quickly backtracked to the Temple and located him sitting happily in the presence of sages, conversing and asking questions about Torah.

He surely appeared a promising chap to those religious leaders as he entertained them with beyond-his-years insights. Maybe someone remarked, "He will one day make a fine rabbi." *Perhaps*, those listening thought, *he'll even rise to prominence as one of his people's premier thinkers.*

With this memory in mind, flash forward to the moment of Jesus' second temptation. One couldn't symbolically rise any higher than Jesus has in this surreal moment as he surveys the landscape below from atop the Temple.

Then Satan raises the stakes by proposing a litmus test, a chance for Jesus to confirm his identity as God's beloved

Son. "'He will command his angels concerning you,'" says the devil, quoting Psalm 91. "'On their hands they will bear you up, lest you strike your foot against a stone.'"[5]

Jesus knows well the ancient Hebrew prayer from which Satan draws his words:

> He who dwells in the shelter of the Most High
>    will abide in the shadow of the Almighty. . . .

> A thousand may fall at your side,
>    ten thousand at your right hand,
>    but it will not come near you.[6]

All these things and more are true, so says the psalmist, if you live a life pleasing to the Lord.

> [God] will command his angels concerning you
>    to guard you in all your ways.
> On their hands they will bear you up,
>    lest you strike your foot against a stone.[7]

According to the test, if Jesus leaps from the Temple, and if God's angels catch him, Jesus will prove that God is pleased with him, because the psalm promises divine protection to the one who puts his trust in God. If Jesus is who the Voice claimed he is, he should have no problem jumping from the Temple because God will send angels to intervene.

That's a lot of pressure, to perform such a stunt to garner such approval. Who can fathom what goes through Jesus' mind in that moment? Perhaps, as he gazes on the city below, he sees the trails that he'd traversed as a child heading to the Temple. Perhaps he imagines himself sitting with those sages long ago, speaking about Torah, discussing the very psalm that now rattles around in his brain. Or perhaps he contemplates all the good that he could do for the people were he to successfully leap from the Temple. If others learned of his feat, they'd follow him anywhere, and he'd advance God's Kingdom like no leader ever had.

We don't know all that went through Jesus' mind, but as he speaks the words "'You shall not put the Lord your God to the test'"[8] and steps away from the temptation to perform for approval, we know who he has in mind: Moses and the people of Israel.

The Israelites were ready to stone Moses, the man who called forth plagues on their Egyptian captors, whose staff parted the Red Sea, and who led them through wilderness as manna fell from the heavens for four decades.

Yet none of the miracles were enough to convince the people to trust him. When their forty-year trek through the wilderness concluded, they set up camp at Rephidim. And, as the story goes in Exodus 17, "There was no water for the people to drink." Then the people argued with Moses, telling him, "Give us water to drink."

Moses responded, "Why do you quarrel with me? Why do you test the LORD?"

But the people pressed hard on him, to the point that he feared for his life. They bickered, "Why did you bring us up out of Egypt, to kill us and our children and our livestock with thirst?"

Imagine that you're Moses. Hear the accusations: "Why did *you* bring us up out of Egypt?" sounds a lot different in the ear than "Why did *God* bring us up out of Egypt?"

As his approval ratings plummeted, Moses turned to the Lord and asked, "What shall I do with this people? They are almost ready to stone me." The Lord replied, "Behold, I will stand before you there on the rock at Horeb, and you shall strike the rock, and water shall come out of it, and the people will drink."

Moses did what God commanded, and he named the place Massah, meaning "testing," and Meribah, meaning "quarreling." He gave the place these names because, as the narrator tells us, the people tested God by saying, "Is the LORD among us or not?"[9]

If you have children, or if you've ever been around children whose parents didn't give them what they wanted when they wanted it, you've likely heard the little tyrants bark at the adults something like "You don't love me. If you loved me, you'd give me what I want."

My children said similar things when they were younger.

If they were standing inside our home when they blurted such heresies, I'd ask them to turn on a water faucet and I'd say, "Your mother and I paid the water bill this month, and we're not charging you anything, yet . . ." or I'd ask them to open the pantry and tell them, "You're welcome." That was usually enough to shut them up for a while.

It's easy for children to take for granted the provisions they've received, and to some degree, as a parent, you want this to happen. You don't want children concerned about the water bill or whether the pantry will be stocked. You don't want them thinking about the mortgage or rent, car repairs, taxes, and pest control. You want them to enjoy the innocence of youth. But you also want them to be aware that the freedoms and provisions enjoyed come at the cost of someone else sacrificing on their behalf because you don't want them to grow into entitled adults.

You want them to have the awareness that you love them and that you're doing what's best for them. Sometimes you won't give them everything they want when they want it, but to the best of your ability, you'll always seek to give them what they need when they need it. This is part of an unspoken agreement—a covenant, if you will—between parents and children in a healthy, normal relationship.

So when children say those painful words—"You don't love me. If you loved me, you'd give me what I want"—as a parent, you say to yourself, *If they only knew how much I loved them, and if they only knew all the blessings they have in their lives, they'd never say such things.* But then you think, *They're just children. One day they'll understand.*

Like unaware, ungrateful children, the children of Israel had a difficult time appreciating the goodness of God in their lives. Regardless of how many times the Lord metaphorically turned on the faucet to show them that the water bill had been paid and that he could be trusted—plagues on their oppressors, deliverance from Egypt, parting of the Red Sea, manna falling from the heavens, and so on—at the first sign of adversity, they questioned God's sovereign, parental abilities. "Is the LORD among us or not?" they cried when they lacked water, putting the Lord to the test "though they had seen [his] work."[10]

*Though they had seen his work.* Though the Israelites had seen the Lord deliver time and again, they did not trust. They needed more proof that God would uphold his end of the covenant.

How many times did God need to prove himself? As the story of the children of Israel unfolds, we learn the answer: just once more. For the unbelieving heart, the answer is always just once more.

+

On occasion, I find myself telling hunting stories from when I was a boy. I'm unsure whether people enjoy hearing them, but I enjoy telling them, and so I do. I love to tell one of them in particular because it encapsulates so many of the others.

One afternoon when I was in my teens, I rode the bus from school to my grandparents' house. I asked my grandmother for my grandfather's shotgun and some buckshot ammo, and I carried their 12 gauge into the woods to sit alone by a tree. After a couple of hours, with only minutes of sunlight remaining, the largest buck I had ever encountered slipped through the thicket and made his way toward me.

I stealthily raised my weapon, drew a deep and silent breath, steadied my pulse, aimed at the behemoth, fired my shot, and missed altogether. When I returned to my grandparents' house, my grandmother asked me if I'd killed anything because she heard the shot. I told her that I'd missed.

That's it. That's the story. But it's always interesting to me what people focus on when I tell that story. It's not that I missed the deer but that my parents allowed me, a teenager, to venture into the woods alone with a weapon. What sort of parent allows a child to do such a thing?

My parents, it turns out. And while I don't recommend that other parents permit such activities, I've come to appreciate the free-range childhood they allowed, which shaped me and formed my character.

But I need to tell the rest of the story—or more accurately, the story before the story. How before I missed the largest buck I've ever seen, my father took me hunting hundreds of times, from the time I could hold a pellet gun. How he taught me to hold the gun properly and safely, to dislodge a jammed bullet, to shoot only when I was certain I wouldn't hit an unintended target, to track my way home through the woods should I ever lose my way, and much more besides. This story carries with it all the other stories.

All those untold stories—stories engrained in the fabric of my imagination and embedded in my character—were what allowed my father to trust me alone in the woods. I'd proven to him time and again that I could be trusted. Only after I, his son, passed a thousand little tests in his presence did he allow me to sit in solitude in the deep woods. But even in his absence, I carried something of my father's presence with me. He'd invested himself in me.

*A good father tests his son not because he doubts him but because he believes in him.*

A good father tests his son not because he doubts him but because he believes in him.

But a good son never tests his father.

And this is what's so disturbing about the story of Israel—often referred to as God's son in Scripture—putting God to the test. "Is the LORD among us or not?" is not a question at all, really. It's a statement, a belief that the Father needed to prove his trustworthiness and competence, his nearness to them and his ability to provide for them, though they had seen his works.

The children of Israel reversed the roles of parent and child. The parent tests the child; the child does not test the parent.

And now we can see why Jesus responded to the second temptation the way he did: "You shall not put the Lord your

God to the test."[11] He understood that the Son does not test the Father. No, the Father tests the Son, and he does this to reveal what the Son's made of, to see whether he will remain true to the family ways.

But more than this, the Father tests the Son to help the Son understand what he's made of. When the Son understands, he will not feel the need to prove himself in the face of future tests. The Son's confidence will be based on the Father's belief in him; he will know that he has everything he needs to succeed because the Father has already put him through the paces. In other words, the Son will learn to trust himself—his instincts, discernment, abilities—because the Father trusts him. And this trusting in himself flows directly from his trust in his Father.

Jesus didn't reject the opportunity to leap from the Temple because he was afraid his Father wouldn't or couldn't command angels to catch him. He refused to leap from the Temple because he knew that, even though his Father could command angels to catch him, that's not how a Son treats a Father who's proven time and again that he can be trusted. Their bond was strong; their trust in one another was firm. There was nothing to prove, neither for the Father nor for the Son.

✦ ✦

Though middle school is far behind me, I carried that insecure little boy—worried about his skinny legs, his skinny abilities, his skinny competence—with me throughout much of my adult life. To this day, I still hear him asking me whether he's enough.

Sometimes I remind him of all the times he was alone in the woods and made it out alive. Sometimes I remind him of the times he thought he couldn't make it—through work challenges, health scares, financial stresses—but with God's help, he did.

Sometimes he's convinced, but sometimes he isn't. Sometimes he still wants to leap from the various temples in his life, altars he's erected to his own success, to prove to everyone how high he's climbed. "Look at my house in the perfect neighborhood," he cries. "Look at my job title; look at my stunning performance—my degrees, my gorgeous wife, my whip-smart children, my undeniable greatness!"

Sometimes he dazzles onlookers with his stellar performance. But every time he succeeds at performing for the sake of approval, something inside him shrivels. He feels himself placing a piece of his identity into other people's hands. You'd think he'd learn, but alas, some lessons take a lifetime to master.

I used to berate that little boy inside of me with his longing for approval, but now I have compassion for him. I know that he's after something good and healthy, that he's seeking to meet a valid need for approval, but that sometimes he gets confused and seeks that approval in the eyes of others instead of in the eyes of God. I know he's burning a lot of energy, and that even when he succeeds in his mission, he fails his soul.

And I know that the little boy inside of me who performs

for approval is not alone. If we pay attention, we'll discover a little piece of that child inside all of us. And if we slow down enough, we can let ourselves be curious about how we meet our need for approval. What do we do to prove to ourselves that we measure up, that we have what it takes? How do we—in more ways than we'd care to admit—answer the question *Am I enough?*

And who, or what, is part of answering this question for you? Your children, with their perfect obedience in the presence of other parents, or their stellar performance at school or on the athletic field? Your spouse or partner, by making you feel worthy of love? Your job and the salary you earn?

Or, to ask the question another way: Who or what has become your god?

Whatever we turn to for an answer to the question *Am I enough?* holds the power of our identity in its hands. Whatever we turn to for an answer to this question is forced to become something to us and for us that it was never intended to become. When a person, role, object, et cetera becomes a source of validation and approval for us, it becomes a slave to our egos and is never free to be who or what it truly was intended to be. We use it rather than love it. We exhaust its energy rather than steward it. It becomes a means to meet our need for approval, and so it becomes an object we use for our own gratification.

> Whatever we turn to for an answer to the question *Am I enough? holds the power of our identity in its hands.*

But when we find our approval in the Father's love—the sort of love that never asks us to prove, just once more, our worthiness in order to receive validation—we can finally say, and believe, the words *I am enough*. The Father's love lacks nothing and needs nothing from us. The Father proved his love for us once and for all by sending his only begotten Son into the world to reveal the full essence of his character. And this love is free—no performance necessary.

When we stop performing, we come home to ourselves. We accept ourselves. We embrace the goodness of our life as it is, not as it could be.

But how do we do this? How do we shift from a mindset of performing for approval to this place of deep acceptance that transcends our performance? By adopting one of the core mindsets that strengthened Christ against this temptation: gratefulness.

# INVITATION:
# OPEN YOUR HEART
# IN GRATITUDE

ANYONE WHO ENTERS the Masters Tournament ticket lottery knows that the chances of winning tickets are abysmal. It's the rarest ticket in all of sports. You can inherit tickets or buy them on the aftermarket (which may or may not be legal). Or you must win the ticket lottery.

Finally, after nearly two decades of entering, my name was drawn, granting me four tickets to one day of the tournament. But I nearly missed the opportunity entirely.

Each year in the summertime, applicants receive an email from The Masters. It opens with words that break your heart: "We regret . . ." You stop reading. You go back to work. You enter again next year. After decades of heartbreak, your heart breaks a little less each time. You expect rejection, but still, you muster hope that maybe this year you'll win.

I was in a staff meeting when one of my colleagues said that he'd received his annual heartbreak email. I checked email on my phone, saw something from The Masters, opened it, scanned it, and went about my business.

The usual rejection.

After work, a text notification from a friend appeared on my phone: *Didn't win tickets this year. You?* I opened my email to send a screenshot of my rejection email and commiserate—and that's when my legs went weak, and I squealed like a stuck pig.

You might have seen those tests where sentences are filled with misspelled words and somehow your brain still sees what it wants to see and reads the words as though they were spelled properly. How this works I have no clue, but essentially you see what you're looking for, what you've been conditioned to see.

Decades of rejection caused me to see "We are pleased to inform . . ." as "We regret . . ." I'd won the lottery, and I nearly threw away the gift I'd received because I didn't recognize that I'd received a gift.

After I calmed down and invited three people to join me at The Masters, I considered my good fortune. And then I wondered just how much of my life is spent expecting rejection or anticipating the worst—meanwhile overlooking the innumerable gifts that have passed me by unaware.

What is gratefulness? "The Hebrew term for gratitude is *hakarat ha'tov*, which means, literally, 'recognizing the good.'"[1] It's the idea that goodness is already present in life, and our invitation is to recognize this goodness.

Monk and author David Steindl-Rast is widely regarded as the most grateful person alive. He's so grateful that scientists have studied his brain to better

> Goodness is already present in life, and our invitation is to recognize this goodness.

understand the effects of gratefulness on a neurobiological level. He says, "Everything is [a] gift. The degree to which we are awake to this truth is the measure of our gratefulness. And gratefulness is the measure of our aliveness."[2]

According to Steindl-Rast, if we're not grateful, we're not truly awake to the lives we are living. We're skimming the surface of our own existence. Like me opening the email and not properly interpreting its contents, we don't comprehend the goodness right in front of us because we default to seeing only the disappointments. And while we must reckon with the inevitable pain and suffering that the human experience entails, viewing life as a gift reframes our hardship and strengthens our resolve to carry on.

As poetic and enticing as this sounds, what does gratefulness have to do with the second temptation of Christ—to perform for approval? It's not obvious at first, but when you really dig into the backstory, the story of Israel that we studied in the previous chapter, the connection becomes more apparent.

You'll recall that when the children of Israel forgot all that God had done for them in the wilderness, they put the Lord to the test, quarrelling with Moses about their lack of water. This was a grievous error, which Psalm 95 memorializes as a warning: "Today, if you hear his voice, do not harden your hearts, as at . . . Massah in the wilderness, when your fathers put me to the test and put me to the proof, *though they had seen my work*."[3]

Because the Israelites failed to appreciate how God had acted on their behalf before, they failed to believe that God would continue to meet their needs. Their lack of gratitude led to a failure to trust God's future provision. Their hearts became hard and their spirits rebellious. This moment of testing God at Massah would haunt them for generations and take on legendary status.

*The Book of Legends* contains fascinating stories from the Jewish tradition. One of them speaks to this very moment, holding a powerful insight related to gratitude and the second temptation.

In the legend, Rabbi Levi tells a story to illustrate the discipline Israel received for testing the Lord:

> What parable applies here to Israel? The parable of a child who was perched on his father's shoulders [in the marketplace]. Each time the child saw a desirable object, he said to his father, "Buy it for me," and his father bought it for him the first time, the second time, and the third time. While they were walking,

the child saw his father's friend and asked him,
"Have you seen my daddy?" The father spoke
sharply to his son, "Silly boy, you are riding astride
my shoulder, whatever you want I buy for you, and
yet you ask this man, 'Have you seen my daddy?'"[4]

Gratefulness is the mindset that makes us aware that we
are riding astride the Father's shoulder. When we fail to see
the goodness of life and all that God has given us, when we
take for granted his many blessings and benevolence toward
us, we're prone to grumble and complain and put him to the
test. We demand signs from him to prove his love for us. We
resort to if/then negotiations: *If you love me, then you will . . .*
or *If I act worthily, then you should . . .* We become like the
petulant child who cannot
discern his father's nearness
because he has not recognized
his father's goodness.

> Gratefulness is the mindset
> that makes us aware that
> we are riding astride
> the Father's shoulder.

What's more, if we can't
see God's goodness *toward*
us, we'll never see God's
goodness *in* us. And if we can't see God's goodness in us,
we'll never cease to perform for approval. We will never feel
like we are enough if we don't understand that the Source
of all life is enough. When we perceive God as lacking
something, then we lack something too. When God fails
to meet expectations, how will we ever measure up to our
own standards?

But when gratefulness opens our hearts to being satisfied by God's goodness, no other opinion, accomplishment, or acclaim matters.

✝

For all its benefits in guarding us against the second temptation, gratefulness is also a very practical means to a life of flourishing. The philosopher Cicero claimed that gratitude is "the mother of all other remaining virtues," encouraging the development of "patience, humility, and wisdom."[5] Explorations into the science of gratitude affirm that gratefulness leads to enhanced overall health, healthier hearts, decreased anxiety and depression, participation in healthy activities, decreased risk of substance abuse, better sleep, deepened spirituality, and more.[6]

Beyond that, gratefulness literally reshapes our brains. UCLA's Mindfulness Awareness Research Center reports, "having an attitude of gratitude changes the molecular structure of the brain, keeps the gray matter functioning, and makes us healthier and happier. When you feel happiness, the central nervous system is affected. You are more peaceful, less reactive, and less resistant."[7]

When we speak of having the mind of Christ as our aim, perhaps we're asking for more than we know. Have you considered that, grateful as he was, Jesus might have had the most enviable brain in human history?

If on one hand, gratefulness leads to better health and well-being and is the mother of other virtues, then on the other hand, ingratitude is the father of many vices, moves us away from well-being, and can become a contributing factor in our downfalls.[8] There's a cost to ingratitude, as another Jewish legend makes clear:

> When Abraham's guests wished to bless him for his generosity, he would say to them: "Has the food you have eaten been provided by me? You should thank, praise and bless He who spoke the world into being!" If they refused, Abraham would demand payment for the food they had eaten. "How much do I owe you?" they would ask. "A jug of wine is one *folarin*," Abraham would say; "a pound of meat, one *folarin*; a loaf of bread, one *folarin*." When the guest would protest these exorbitant prices, Abraham would counter: "Who supplies you with wine in the middle of the desert? Who supplies you with meat in the desert? Who supplies you with bread in the desert?" When the guest would realize the predicament he was in, he would relent and proclaim: "Blessed be the G-d of the world, from whose providence we have eaten."[9]

I would love to convert the ancient value of a *folarin* into contemporary dollars so that the story would have a more shocking effect, but despite much research, I cannot locate any information on this ancient form of payment. But perhaps that's the point—if you have to ask how much a *folarin* is worth, you can't afford it!

So if gratefulness is the preferred, healthy mindset and ingratitude is a block to well-being, then we'd do well to consider what inhibits us from being more grateful. Anthropologist, filmmaker, and writer Alan Morinis draws upon the teachings of Rabbi Bachya ibn Pakuda, who identified three reasons we sometimes lack a perspective of gratefulness. First, "we are too absorbed in worldly things and in the enjoyment of them." Second, "we are so used to our gifts that we don't even really see them any more." And third, "we are so focused on the travails and afflictions we suffer in this world that we forget that both our very being and all we own are among the good things that have been gifted to us."[10]

All three reasons for ingratitude share one common element: a skewed perspective of reality. Perspective is vital in cultivating gratefulness. In *Man's Search for Meaning*, Holocaust survivor and psychiatrist Viktor Frankl offers this powerful insight: "Everything can be taken from a man but one thing: the last of the human freedoms—to choose one's attitude in any given set of circumstances, to choose one's own way."[11]

Whatever goodness or trouble comes our way, we can choose our perspective. Even in suffering, we can search for something for which we can be grateful.

But "what if I cannot recognize the given as a blessing?" asks Bro. David Steindl-Rast. "What if it is not sunshine that pours down on us, but hailstones like hammer-blows? What if it is acid rain? Here, again, the gift within the gift is opportunity. I have the opportunity, for example, to do something about that acid rain, face the facts, inform myself about the causes, go to their roots, alert others, band together with them for self-help, for protest. By taking each opportunity as it is offered, I show myself grateful."[12]

When we don't necessarily feel gratitude, when life is full of hardship and suffering, we can still search for the opportunity to be grateful *in* all things, as we seek to achieve the level of gratefulness prescribed by the apostle Paul in Ephesians: to give thanks *for* all things.[13] I'll confess, I'm not there yet, and if you're not there yet either, we'll trust that there's room for us to grow together.

That said, nobody should ever tell you when and how to be grateful. Nobody should tell you how you should view any given situation, for nobody has the information, experience, and insight that you alone possess. But if the wisdom that we've inherited through the ages is of any value, it seems that embracing a mindset of gratefulness is a healthier path in life than bitterness. As writer and critic Alphonse Karr so eloquently quipped, "We can complain because rosebushes have thorns, or rejoice because thorns have roses."[14]

If Bro. David Steindl-Rast is the most grateful person alive (age ninety-six as of this writing), Jesus surely is the most grateful person who has ever lived. In a mystery beyond human comprehension, Scripture tells us that the entire cosmos was created by means of the Christ,[15] and yet he offered thanks to God for his everyday sustenance, even for a handful of bread.

Jesus' gratefulness became a hallmark of his identity, particularly related to the way he handled bread. In fact, Jesus became so well known for the way he handled bread that, following his resurrection, his handling of bread was what revealed his identity to people who did not at first recognize him.

Luke 24 recalls a time when two people were walking to a village named Emmaus, talking about Jesus' crucifixion. It's then that Jesus appeared to them, "but their eyes were kept from recognizing him."[16] A conversation ensued about the preceding days' events as the two explained to Jesus their shattered hopes that he was the Messiah, as it had now been three days since his execution.

Then—and this absolutely astounds me—Jesus rebukes them for their lack of belief and proceeds to interpret from the Scriptures the things concerning how the Messiah must suffer, beginning with Moses and making his way through the Prophets. And still they did not perceive that it was Jesus who was standing with them. They did, however, have enough discernment to realize that they desired to learn more, and so they pleaded with him to stay with them. And he did.

"When he was at table with them," Luke tells us, "he took the bread and blessed and broke it and gave it to them. And their eyes were opened, and they recognized him. And he vanished from their sight."[17] They arose that very hour, returned to Jerusalem, and shared the news that they had met with Jesus, "and how he was known to them in the breaking of the bread."[18]

It wasn't Jesus' interpretation of the Scriptures about himself that opened their eyes to his identity but rather the way he handled bread. Whenever Jesus handled bread throughout Scripture, he handled it the same way—he took it, gave thanks for it, broke it, and gave it.[19] Something about this process opened their eyes, and they understood who he truly was.

When we're grateful, perhaps people will discern the presence of Christ among us, too. Perhaps, as we're grateful, the disappointment and dejection that others feel, like those two sojourners on the road to Emmaus, will dissolve in our very presence. And perhaps gratefulness will help us discern that Christ is nearer to each of us than we realize and longs to be in our presence as much as we long to be in his.

Gratefulness opens our eyes to the goodness of God. It focuses on what God has done, not on what we wish God would do. And over time, gratefulness opens our eyes to the goodness of God within us. It helps us focus on who we are and what God is doing in and through us, rather than who we are not and our inabilities.

Gratefulness guards us against the temptation to perform for approval. Because God and what God gives is enough, *we* are enough. There is nothing to prove, nobody to impress.

When I finally entered the hallowed grounds of Augusta National Golf Course for The Masters, before I walked through the corridor toward the first tee, before my feet trod on the most perfect blades of grass anywhere on God's green earth, I paused and stood still. I opened my eyes as wide as I could. I breathed deep of the Augusta morning breeze. A haze of pastel pink kissed the crest line of Georgia pines. A delicate fog wafted through the space between the scoreboard and the first tee. And my heart grew strangely warm as gratitude flooded my awareness.

It's unlikely that I'll ever again set foot on the glorious grounds of Augusta National Golf Course. But that doesn't matter to me now because I have a photo that reminds me of my once-in-a-lifetime trip. Anytime I want to experience that sense of gratefulness, I glance at a four-by-six-inch photo of me with my brother, my friend, and my father all standing shoulder to shoulder.

My father took off a couple of days of work to make the trip. He's hardly taken off a day of work during the workweek in his life, so for him to relax and unwind and do nothing but eat pimento-cheese sandwiches was a real gift to him. But really, giving him a ticket was a gift to myself.

I have dozens of friends who would have eagerly accepted a ticket, and I nearly took someone on the trip other than my father. My father has played perhaps as many rounds of golf in his lifetime as he has digits on one hand. He's a woodworker, a fisherman, a fixer-of-all-things, but rarely a golfer.

But this trip wasn't about golf; it was about gratitude. This was a small way that I could express gratefulness for the thousands of hours—many unseen and unbeknownst to me—that he'd worked and provided for me. This was about letting my father know that, though I might not have seen all his efforts, I wasn't unaware of his goodness toward me. He never needed to do another thing to express his goodness to me. All he's done will have been enough. He has nothing to prove to me, and I have nothing to prove to him.

I could never repay him for everything he's done. But then again, gratitude isn't really about repaying anyone for anything. It's about paying attention to the goodness that surrounds us and having the awareness that, ultimately, it all comes from the good hand of the Lord.

# PRACTICE:
# MEDITATE ON SCRIPTURE

IN MY EARLY DAYS OF MINISTRY, a small group of students in our church was part of a team whose goal was to memorize and recite passages of Scripture. This team wasn't as popular as some of the other teams that formed among students—the dance and drama teams, the tech and worship teams, the greeters, and so on—but they were every bit as committed to their craft.

In their competitions against teams from other churches, they'd sit at long tables, shoulder to shoulder, with the other teams seated likewise, all facing the judge. The judge would cite a Scripture reference, such as Philippians 4:13, and if any player from either team knew it, the player would slam their buzzer Jeopardy-style and then recite the verse when called on. If every word was recited with precision, their team received a point, and at the end of the allotted time, the team with the most points won the competition. Exceptional teams advanced to state- and even national-level competitions.

In our church, other ministry teams often made their way onto the stage at youth group to perform. At some point, one of the Bible trivia team leaders decided that their students deserved a moment to demonstrate their prowess. And since having the team compete against other students in the youth group would be embarrassing for the untrained students, they thought it best to select yours truly as their opposition.

Over time, I have committed to memory a fair amount of Scripture, but nothing compared to these kids. Much of my memorization work bears words like *thee* and *thou*, and they graciously agreed to let my seventeenth-century recitations suffice for the competition, though they used more modern translations. The team was confident that I could even have the Bible opened in front of me and still not stand a chance.

And I didn't. They routed me, at least the first time. The second time, the Bible-trivia master provided me with the Scriptures that would be used ahead of the event. Even after I committed those to memory, I still lost—the students were faster to the buzzers and more precise with their responses. However, this time, the margin of defeat was respectable, and I appeared less like an unwitting fool than before.

Some of these Bible-memory prodigies went on to become pastors and devoted disciples working in various career fields, and I'm confident that they can still recite more Scripture than I can. Others, however, left their faith not long after leaving high school. Still, I can imagine that even to this day, if I were to pass one of them on the street and shout, "Philippians 4:13," these individuals would snap to attention and respond, "I can do all things through [Christ] who strengthens me"—even if they've long since resorted to other means of forming a life and personal identity.

I love these students, now adults, so understand that I don't intend to cast a shadow on them. But here's the point: Any of us can memorize all the Scripture in the Good Book, yet we will miss out on its benefits if we don't transcend simply reading or even memorizing it—if we do not allow it to form our hearts and shape our lives.

Remember, as we've seen in the temptation passage, even the devil memorized Scripture:

Then the devil took him to the holy city and set him on the pinnacle of the temple and said to him, "[Since] you are the Son of God, throw yourself down, *for it is written*,

"'He will command his angels concerning you,'

and

"'On their hands they will bear you up,
    lest you strike your foot against a stone.'"

Jesus said to him, *"Again it is written,* 'You shall not put the Lord your God to the test.'"[1]

In this case of Jesus and the devil quoting Scripture back and forth, the prevailing party is not the one who most accurately recites a passage—they both excel in this manner—but the one who not only memorized it but also allowed it to form a heart for God within him.

While memorization has its place and benefits, meditation is what allows Scripture to sink from our heads to our hearts, and it's from the heart that we speak, act, and learn to see the world.[2] Meditation does more than lodge words in file cabinets in our minds so they're readily available when we need them. Rather, meditation conditions our outlook on the world, posturing us toward gratefulness, positioning us to resist the temptation to perform for approval.

> Meditation is what allows Scripture to sink from our heads to our hearts, and it's from the heart that we speak, act, and learn to see the world.

Meditating on what is true—and Scripture is truth in the highest sense—enables us to properly see the world. We don't wake up in the world one day seeing properly. We have to learn to see; we have to practice. Jesus' practice of Scripture meditation is what enabled him to see through the devil's offers, to live with gratitude, and to resist the temptation to perform for approval.

The word *meditation* sounds an alarm in some Christian minds, evoking images of gurus sitting cross-legged amid chants and incense smoke. When I've taught on Scripture meditation, I've occasionally even been met by pushback, a wariness of anything that seems *Eastern* or *mystical*.

Notwithstanding the reality that the Christian tradition has its origins in the Ancient Near East, and that any religion claiming direct contact with the divine is by definition mystical (personal relationship with Jesus, anyone?), Scripture meditation is a very orthodox practice that has its origins in Scripture itself.

The traditional Christian practice of meditation on Scripture is distinctly different from the image of gurus chanting that I depicted above. Writer and professor Donald Whitney draws helpful distinctions between the Christian practice of Scripture meditation and the forms of meditation that are often "associated with yoga, transcendental meditation, relaxation therapy, or some New Age practice." He writes,

> The kind of meditation encouraged in the Bible
> differs from other kinds of meditation in several
> ways. While some advocate a kind of meditation
> in which you do your best to empty your mind,
> Christian meditation involves filling your mind
> with God and His truth. For some, meditation is
> an attempt to achieve complete mental passivity,

but biblical meditation requires constructive mental activity. Worldly meditation employs visualization techniques intended to "create your own reality." And while Christian history has always had a place for the sanctified use of our God-given imagination in meditation, imagination is our servant to help us meditate on things that are true (see Philippians 4:8). Furthermore, instead of "creating our own reality" through visualization, we link meditation with prayer to God and responsible, Spirit-filled human action to effect changes.[3]

When practiced as Whitney suggests, and as the ancient Christian tradition teaches us, meditation is a safe and healthy practice. And for Jesus, Scripture meditation was not only safe and healthy but also a normal practice, as normal as Sabbath and sacrifice. He stood in a long line of Jews who were commanded to meditate on Scripture. His prayer book, the Psalms, begins with one of many encouragements for Scripture meditation:

> Blessed is the man
>     who walks not in the counsel of the wicked,
> nor stands in the way of sinners,
>     nor sits in the seat of scoffers;
> but his delight is in the law of the LORD,
>     and on his law he meditates day and night.[4]

Scripture meditation grounded God's people in truth, shaping their imaginations and forming their character. It was through Scripture meditation—on their sacred stories and spiritual wisdom—that one generation inherited the mindsets, customs, and practices from the previous generation. When ancient stories were passed from one generation to the next, Israel retained and solidified its identity and its sense of place and meaning in the world.

*When*, however, is vital, for *when they did not* meditate on Scripture, on their core narratives, they failed to remember who they were, and they forgot God's goodness and became ungrateful. They failed at their vocation as the people of God, seeking instead to become like all the other nations of the world. And likewise, when we do not meditate on Scripture, we forget who we are and lose the plot that provides structure, shape, direction, and meaning for our lives.

But when we meditate on Scripture, God's words shape our minds, showing us who we are and who God is. Scripture reminds us that we are not left to our own devices to create, out of whole cloth, some sense of meaningfulness in our lives, to construct our own stories from scratch, for our stories are part of God's story. And it reminds us of God's many blessings in our lives, for which we should remain grateful.

The Trappist monk Thomas Merton encourages us,

We wish to gain a true evaluation of ourselves and of the world so as to understand the meaning of our life as children of God redeemed from sin and death. . . . These are the aims and goals of [meditation].[5]

We need a true evaluation of ourselves. When we immerse our minds and hearts in truth, the silly and flippant arguments and opinions flooding our minds fall silent. We develop a slow and deliberate thoughtfulness, becoming more protected against the temptation to perform for others' approval. No longer do we seek to leap from one metaphorical temple after the next to ensure we measure up. Instead, we grow grateful as we meditate on what is true about God, true about the world, and true about ourselves. We find peace in wisdom, and we find this wisdom as we immerse our minds in the Holy Scriptures.

> *We find peace in wisdom, and we find this wisdom as we immerse our minds in the Holy Scriptures.*

While I'd prefer you think you're sitting at the feet of a master Scripture meditator, the truth is, my meditating mind can resemble a tree full of preadolescent, caffeinated, hyperactive orangutans. I'm a work in process, and I'm writing not from a place of meditation mastery but from what I know to be true based on my experience and the experiences of trustworthy guides.

The best way that I've come to think about meditation is that it simply means to think deeply about something. You can meditate on a candle, a fingernail, a box of cereal, a paper clip, a conversation you had, a word, a song, a trip you'll take, a friend you miss, a fear that grips you—anything. From this perspective, whether you realize it or not, you are already an accomplished meditator. The issue is whether what you are meditating on has beneficial or harmful effects on your soul.

Alan Morinis, again citing Rabbi Bachya ibn Pakuda, illustrates the impact of meditation on the soul:

> The intellect is not the most profound aspect of the soul; it is not the root. But impressions—wholesome as well as unwholesome—gathered in the mind do pass down to the root, and color and shape the soul.[6]

The things we see, the things we think deeply on, imprint in the deepest place of our being and cleanse or taint the well from which flows our words and actions, our dreams and aspirations.

Because we are all indeed proficient meditators, the issue then becomes this: How do we go about meditating on a subject that has the power to shape our souls in healthy ways? Let's consider a few practical guides to Scripture meditation.

First, when we meditate, the goal is not to get through the Scriptures but to get the Scriptures through us.[7] Before we unpack this statement, understand that I am absolutely an advocate of Bible reading and of Bible memorization. I'm a proponent and promoter of the plans that take you through some portion of, or indeed the whole sweep of, Scripture over a defined period, like read-the-Bible-in-a-year plans. These have their place and are beneficial. We need to read through the whole of Scripture to gain a perspective of how its various pieces work and weave together.

But when we meditate, we are not reading for information—we are reading for transformation. And transformation is slow and deep work. We're not seeking to merely interpret the text but to allow it to interpret the deep places of our hearts and lives to us. We're not even seeking to master the text but rather to be mastered by it.

Seventeenth-century French mystic Madame Guyon illustrates this point well:

> If you read quickly, it will benefit you little. You will be like a bee that merely skims the surface of a flower. Instead, in this new way of reading with prayer, you must become as the bee who penetrates into the *depths* of the flower. You plunge deeply within to remove its deepest nectar.[8]

To take the plunge, we need to give ourselves permission to sit with just a few lines, or perhaps even just a word or two, and to think deeply about them. We allow this small portion of Scripture that we have found meaningful to roll around in our hearts and minds like a cough drop in our mouths. When we do, the taste lingers long. Scripture continues its work as we go throughout our days, available for us to draw upon as needed.

Second, Scripture reading is done with the eyes, but Scripture meditation is done with the ears. I'm not referring to listening to Scripture being read aloud but rather to the mindset and awareness with which we approach Scripture as we seek to meditate on it. Eugene Peterson writes,

> Listening and reading are not the same thing. They involve different senses. In listening we use our ears; in reading we use our eyes. We listen to the sound of a voice; we read marks on paper. . . . Listening is an interpersonal act; it involves two or more people in fairly close proximity. . . . The listener is required to be attentive to the speaker and is more or less at the speaker's mercy. . . . When I read a book the book does not know if I am paying attention or not; when I listen to a person the person knows very well whether I am paying attention or not. In listening, another initiates the process; when I read I initiate the process. . . . I can read by myself; I cannot listen by myself. In listening the speaker is in charge; in reading the reader is in charge.[9]

Peterson goes on to explain that listening to Scripture, of course, presupposes that we read Scripture.[10] While we cannot listen to Scripture without reading it (or having it read to us), we can read it without listening to it. And when we do, we miss out on the depth of transformational work that

Scripture can do as it works its way to the roots of our souls, alive, active, and transforming us all the way down.

Third, an important goal of Scripture meditation is application—to live it out in your daily life and interactions. We're not meditating just so we can have *aha!* moments of insight or revelation (though we're open to them); we're seeking to have our minds renewed and our souls transformed so we can live as more effective disciples, resisting the temptations that make their way to us.

Joshua 1:8 admonishes us, "This Book of the Law shall not depart from your mouth, but you shall meditate on it day and night, so that you may be careful to do according to all that is written in it." We leave our time of meditation seeking to embody and practice the truth that captivated our attention.

When we meditate on Scripture, we come to it ready to be changed, seeking to hear what it has to say to us personally so that we can live it out publicly. We're not coming to it with the intention of getting the whole story, or covering large amounts of the text in a sitting, or analyzing it. We're coming to it with the slow and inefficient purpose of an intimate listening. As we listen, we do not leave the words on the page. We take what we have heard, and we move forward into our days.

✦

I was reading the opening chapters of Matthew's Gospel when a phrase I'd read many times leapt from the page. Matthew was chronicling the events surrounding Jesus' birth, including the magi visiting and lavishing gifts on the Christ child.

When the magi left, an angel instructed Joseph in a dream to flee with Mary and the child to Egypt. Joseph obeyed the angel's command and stayed there until the death of Herod, who sought the infant's life. "This," Matthew tells us, "was to fulfill what the Lord had spoken by the prophet, 'Out of Egypt I called my son.'"[11]

*Out of Egypt I called my son* arrested my attention. I stopped reading, closed the book, and thought about just those few words. Egypt—I'd always thought of Egypt as the place where God's people were oppressed, but Egypt in this case is where the Son of God was preserved. And then my mind meandered to how another Joseph, back in Genesis, found himself in Egypt—also because of a dream. Egypt was where God's people were preserved, and Egypt was where they were severely oppressed.[12]

Egypt—the place of preservation and oppression. I thought about this for a while, how the places I often experience the most discomfort are the very places where God is growing, preparing, and preserving me for what's next. And then two very painful moments from my life came to mind. Each moment represented a time when I knew God had called me to a place and had given me an assignment, and yet I experienced profound pain in the process. Previously, I could hardly think about either of those places without pain surfacing. But in this moment, I considered how God had grown and stretched and transformed my life in ways that would not have been possible had I not gone through those experiences. I began to reflect on the goodness of God that transpired in my life in those painful places. These were my Egypts—my places of preservation *and* suffering.

This moment of Scripture meditation didn't take away the pain of those seasons, but it did expand my focus so I could recall the good hand of the Lord on my life. I began to see that season of my story through a broader, healthier lens that was shaded with Scripture. I became grateful for it.

When we meditate, we interpret Scripture through the lens of our experiences, and as we do, God's Word interprets the experiences of our lives back to us—reframing them in light of God's work as depicted in Scripture. We don't just read the Bible; the Bible reads us.[13] It forms us. It gives our stories meaning and trajectory and the sense of purpose they deserve. Scripture meditation helps us see the world with a grateful, confident mind—the mind of Christ.

Jesus' imagination was a key part of his resistance against the Temptations. When tempted to turn stones to bread, he recalled Israel's manna moment. When seduced to throw himself from the Temple, he remembered Israel's Massah moment. These moments came quickly to him because they were embedded in his memory. He'd sat with them, mulled them over as he walked and talked and laid down to rest. Day and night for his entire life, he'd marinated in these stories, and when the time came for him to be tested, the

Scriptures came to life before his eyes because they were hidden in his heart.

Jesus had somewhat of an advantage over us, and not just because he was the only begotten Son of God. His culture was saturated in Scripture. Law, commerce, customs all had Scripture as their reference point. While we might encounter a person of faith here and there during our day, or happen upon a Scripture reference on a billboard or business sign, the current of culture is drifting further downstream from having Scripture as its source of inspiration. This doesn't leave us without hope, and we should not be discouraged. Rather, our cultural reality should compel us to become more diligent in meditating on the truths of Scripture, as they are our greatest defense against whatever seeks to lead us from the Way of Jesus.

But where are we to begin? Perhaps you already have a trusted practice for Scripture meditation. Maybe you've encountered the ancient Christian practice of *sacred reading*, often referred to as *lectio divina*. Or, if you're fortunate, maybe you've heard of the methods developed by Saint Ignatius of Loyola, how he trained disciples in the art of gospel contemplation. Then there are more contemporary aids, such as *The Prayerful Reading Bible* based on *The Message* by my hero Eugene Peterson. A simple internet search will provide you with references to each of these practices and resources.[14]

I'm tempted, as I reference each of these resources, to offer some instructions on how each of them work. But I'd be lying to you if I told you that these practices were what

I've found most beneficial, and I committed to tell you the truth. Here's the truth: The way I've come to think deeply about Scripture, to meditate on it, doesn't bear any formal label or Latin words. It's not based on any methodology I've been taught. It's not sophisticated or difficult. It's so simple that I'm ashamed to admit it, wishing I had something more enlightening to offer.

I just read the Bible, slowly. I'm a slow reader anyhow, but when I read the Bible to meditate, I drop it down another gear.

And when I come to a word or phrase that piques my interest or arouses my soul, I stop and sit with it for a moment. I pay attention to the thoughts and images that come to mind. Sometimes I'll grab my journal and write about what surfaces. Sometimes I'll pick up my guitar and softly strum and just think about the passage of Scripture. And sometimes I'll just underline it and move on.

I'm not that structured. Sorry if that disappoints you, but I'm not (and the second temptation has encouraged me not to care what you think anyhow). But I can tell you this: I think about Scripture a lot. I love it. I trust it. I wrestle with it. I question it. I use it in conversations, working it in not by quoting it but by saying it in my own words. There's nothing else in all the world like it.

And sometimes, when I least expect it, when I'm doubting or struggling, worrying, or rushing from one thing to the next, that passage of Scripture will stir in my heart and wave at me as if to say, *Remember me?*

Remember. That's what Scripture meditation allows me to do. It helps me remember who I am. It helps me remember that I stand in a long line of people whose imaginations were shaped by the same stories—ancient stories I can trust, bearing deeper wisdom than the stories that flit and flitter across our screens. It helps me remember on whose shoulder I sit too.

> Scripture meditation ... helps me remember who I am. It helps me remember that I stand in a long line of people whose imaginations were shaped by the same stories ... It helps me remember on whose shoulder I sit too.

Most of all, it reminds me of all God has done for me and helps me be grateful. And when I'm grateful, I accept myself for who I am and my life for what it is.

# Do I Matter?

# TEMPTATION:
# CONTROL THROUGH POWER

---

AS AN OLDER TEENAGER, I worked at a golf course, where I cleaned carts and clubs. As young as I was, I was below virtually everyone else on the food chain, which meant I answered to practically everyone. Most of my supervisors were great. One of them wasn't. He often belittled me in ways that cut to the core.

I recall one afternoon when Archie, Peyton, and Eli Manning—three of the most famous NFL quarterbacks in recent history—came to play our course. They had one of the last tee times of the day, so all I had left to do was clean a few carts after the golfers completed play. At the time, Eli was still in high school; Archie was already a football legend;

and Peyton was a Heisman hopeful and had not yet won the Super Bowl or discovered his true calling as an actor in commercials.

A sports fan, I was in awe. So when one of them said, "We only have three. Do you want to be our fourth player?" I nearly peed myself.

"Um, yeah, let me go ask my supervisor if I can play," I told them. But already my heart was sinking—I knew who was in charge that day.

I raced to check in with him. "Hey, most of the carts are in, and we don't have any more tee times. Do you care if I go play a quick nine with the Mannings? They asked me; I didn't ask them. I'll wash all the carts when I get back and make sure everything is tidied up." My youthful enthusiasm surely sounded not so much like a request as a plea—I really wanted to play golf with these guys.

"No," he replied. "You need to stay here and wash carts as they come in."

I sulked back to the parking lot and told them that I could not play. When they returned their cart after the round, I removed the scorecard from the steering wheel and put it in my pocket. Eli, Archie, Peyton—three names on three lines. I wished I could have fired that supervisor and added my name on the fourth line of that scorecard.

Maybe that supervisor was right in telling me that we needed someone at the cart barn. I was a kid; what did I know? Maybe carts needed to be washed one by one as they trickled in, rather than all at once before closing shop. Maybe

I needed to be there in case a member stopped by and needed her clubs.

But this wasn't the first time I wanted to fire this supervisor. I wanted to fire him when he belittled me in front of my coworkers. I wanted to fire him when he made fun of me for my beliefs. I wanted to fire him for the way he made me feel small and powerless.

I didn't have language for it at the time, but now I do: I wanted to fire him because he used his power to control and make me feel insignificant.

But I didn't have any power over him. However, there was someone who did. She was at the very top of the food chain. We called her the Big Boss. And it's taken me more than two decades to appreciate just how incredible a boss she was.

Professional golf—not what you see on television, but rather the professionals who work at golf courses and manage the business of golf—does not have a storied history of women who were head golf professionals working at local golf courses. To this day, male golf professionals grossly outnumber the females, but back then, the number of female professionals paled in comparison even more than it does now.

I had recently quit playing baseball because, as a skinny eighth grader on the high school varsity team, two older, stronger players made it their mission to give me wedgies and stick my head in toilets. I loved baseball and I was good at it, but I hated being afraid every time we had an away game.

Not only did I lose a sport I loved, but I also lost that circle of friendship.

"Do you think you could teach me to play golf?" I asked the Big Boss.

"Sure. Meet me on the driving range after work," she replied. From the first lesson, I was hooked. And she went on to give me countless lessons, all for free. In a little over a year, I went from not knowing how to properly grip a club to being one of the best junior golfers in the area.

I remember those lessons she gave me. But it was a moment in her office that impressed upon me in ways I'll never forget. "Tommy, I need you to do better." She was sternly reprimanding me for poor performance in something I'd done, telling me if I didn't shape up, there would be further consequences.

I was never called into her office again. I shaped up. And I didn't shape up because I was afraid of her. I wasn't afraid of her at all, not like I was afraid of those older boys who bullied me, and not like I was intimidated by that supervisor who belittled me.

> *"Nothing is more useful than power, nothing more frightful."*—RABBI HESCHEL

I shaped up because she was powerful—truly powerful. She saw the best in me and saw my potential, and rather than controlling me with her power, she used her power to make me better and stronger.

That's the power of power—for better or worse.

Rabbi Heschel wrote: "Nothing is more useful than power, nothing more frightful."[1]

At its core, power is good.

I rush to add a *but* to that last sentence, but you've already beaten me to it.

Power is good, *but* people abuse it.

Your mind races to . . .

The boss who wields power in the workplace to manipulate and abuse subordinates and promote himself and his agenda.

The parent who berates her child for the least infraction.

The hard-nosed coach who mercilessly screams at players for poor performance.

The pastor who uses the Good News to make you feel like garbage.

The teacher who spits snide remarks at students who are not behaving properly.

The local government and its agent who enact and implement law for the betterment of some and the detriment of others.

I've surely omitted something, some institution or movement or policy or person.

But you know the stories.

Abuses of power abound.

Power can be destructive.

*But* power can also lead to flourishing.

Because power itself is not the problem.

Power that is used to control—to dominate, destroy, or diminish—is the culprit.

And this is the sort of power Satan offers Jesus in his third temptation.

✦

Jesus surveys the world's kingdoms from atop a tall mountain. Caesar reigns below as Roman statues tower over God's people. They long for a deliverer—one who will ride victoriously through the streets in a chariot dripping with the blood of his enemies. Israel will be restored when Messiah arrives and sets things straight.

Perhaps Jesus thinks to himself, *They need a new Moses.*

And whether he thinks it or not, his countrymen already do. They long for an exodus from their current state of oppression.

Then a voice emerges, the one that has haunted Jesus twice before: "All these I will give you, if you will fall down and worship me."[2]

As I imagine this moment, I wonder if Jesus' mind races to Moses as Israel's leader ascends Sinai.[3]

The mountain is smothered in darkness, trembling, lightning illuminating its craggy contours as thunder peals loudly, striking fear into the hearts of his followers far below. Moses disappears into the fire on the mountain.

The children of Israel grow increasingly fearful. Moses is

gone forty days and nights. They're already anxious, standing in sheer dread of their future. And now, they're afraid for their leader—the man in whom they've invested so much hope.

Is Moses even alive?

In this moment, God himself seems unsafe.

"Make us gods who shall go before us," they implore Aaron, Moses' brother, the closest thing they have to an authority figure.

"Take off the rings of gold," he commands them.

So they lay their treasure plundered from the Egyptians at Aaron's feet, and he fashions a golden calf.

"These are your gods!" the Israelites exclaim.[4]

And the people worship it.

But then Moses descends the mountain with the Law—a wedding ring of sorts, symbolizing the covenant the Almighty offered Israel; tablets bearing God's words, inscribed by God's finger. First among them: *You shall have no other gods before me.*[5]

Moses sees the idolatry. Moses shatters the tablets. Moses is incensed.

He confronts Aaron. He obliterates the golden idol. He grinds it to powder and pours its dust on the water. He forces the people to drink, to satiate their thirst for a god they can control.

And Jesus turns from this memory to the presence leering over his shoulder as it motions to the kingdoms that lie before him, promising the world and control of all its power in exchange for him bowing his knees in worship.

"Be gone, Satan!" Jesus says. "For it is written, 'You shall worship the Lord your God and him only shall you serve.'"[6]

+ +

Sex and landscaping. Oh, and naming exotic animals.

That's it. That's all the first couple—Adam and Eve—had to concern themselves with as the Almighty placed them in the garden in Eden and gave them oversight of the whole project.

And yet the world was not enough. "When you eat of [the fruit] your eyes will be opened, and you will be like God, knowing good and evil," promised the serpent.[7] Eve ate. She shared her snack. Adam ate.

And it was at that moment they realized they were gardening in the nude.

And it was then that they experienced a sense of separation—within themselves, between themselves, and with God.

Adam powers up and blames Eve, who blames the serpent.

And as the years go on, so the misuse of power continues . . .

Cain overtakes and murders Abel . . .

Amnon dominates and rapes Tamar . . .

Genocides . . .

Crusades . . .

Politicians baptizing, weaponizing faith to control followers . . .

All because so long ago, instead of stewarding creation—creatively cultivating God's good world with the power they'd inherited—humankind made it their mission to dominate and control one another.

"Eat [this fruit and] your eyes will be opened, and you will be like God." They already were. They were the very image of God on the earth.

"Bow down and worship me, and the kingdoms of the world are yours." These kingdoms were already Christ's. Everything was created by him and through him.[8]

We already have the thing we seek. It's embedded in our DNA—we are the image bearers, so we don't bow down to any image or anyone or anything but God alone. That's the paradox of the third temptation—the more we clamor for power and control, the less true power and control we possess.

> *The more we clamor for power and control, the less true power and control we possess.*

The invitation that Jesus rejected was the power to control, or said another way, to control by using power. He could have reasoned that gaining such power was in his people's best interest: They needed certainty; they needed deliverance; they needed a real leader amid all the oppression they'd endured.

They needed a new Moses.

But Jesus, his mind clear from fasting and prayer, knew that the way you gain and wield your power matters more than the results achieved by your power. In other words, it's not always about what you do; it's about how you do what you do.

For Jesus, the end did not justify the means. Power that is used to dominate, diminish, and destroy, rather than to seek fulfillment and flourishing, could not bring about the Kingdom vision that burgeoned in his heart.

Jesus was Israel's King. Jesus was the Way to freedom. Jesus was the long-awaited Messiah, who would conquer all enemies who stood in his way. The only problem was, Jesus' Kingdom was not of this world, so the ways and means he used to advance his Kingdom were not of this world. His enemies were not the world's enemies. His thoughts were not the world's thoughts. His view of power was not the world's view of power.

So Satan's offer was of no interest to him.

Power was not something Jesus would seize. True power was something he would receive from God alone—God's power to do God's work in God's way to pursue God's plans.

It had been nearly thirty years since I'd spoken to the Big Boss, the golf professional. I found an article about her on the internet, which mentioned the golf course at which she now worked. I called the course and left a voice mail for her. Several days passed, and I figured she didn't recognize my name or wasn't interested in returning my call. Until one day, when my phone rang with an out-of-state number showing on the screen.

Hearing her voice brought a smile to my face. Warm, inviting, energetic, wise, her tone reminded me why I still cherished memories of her. She told me how her story had unfolded these past three decades. And she told me, now that I was old enough to understand, the difficulty she had faced in those early years as a golf professional.

I could hear a smile in her voice, like she had transformed the struggles she'd faced into something powerful.

"You know, someone should write your story and share it with others," I told her.

"Oh goodness, no. Nobody would ever read it. I'm nothing special," she responded.

"You're special to me," I replied. "You made me feel special, like I had potential. You had no way of knowing what I was going through as a young person, but you treated me with dignity and respect. You really made an impact. And to do what you did as a female golf professional in those days, it's remarkable. And back then, well, it was groundbreaking."

She paused and said, "I don't know what to say. That might be the nicest thing anyone has ever said to me. I really don't think I did anything all that special. I suppose I just tried to treat people the way I hoped they'd treat me."

When you work for the most powerful woman in the room, you hope that's what she's aiming to achieve. Because when that is the case, when that sort of power is wielded with that sort of precision, potential is unleashed, people flourish, and they feel like they matter.

And that's really what's at play here in the third

> *If you're lucky, you might just meet someone who, by their very presence, uses their power to awaken you to the reality that you have power of your own and that you can use it to bring immense good into the world.*

temptation: the question of whether you matter. And while this question can ultimately only be answered in relationship to God, we get to answer it in part for others—to affirm the words that God has already spoken over their lives.

If you're lucky, you might just meet someone who, by their very presence, uses their power to awaken you to the reality that you have power of your own and that you can use it to bring immense good into the world.

And if you're really lucky, you get to be the sort of person who helps others awaken.

You get to be the person who helps other people remember that long ago we were invested with immense creative power and that we get to decide whether to use it to control people or empower them.

Many years after my time on that golf course, I learned a word for this posture and attitude toward power that seeks to fulfill and not negate, to empower and not dominate. A word that describes my Big Boss. And while it's a weak-sounding word, it's the furthest thing from weak.

*Meekness.*

And meekness, incidentally, is the mindset we need to resist the third temptation.

# INVITATION:
# SEEK TO BE MEEK

MY WIFE AND I RECLINED in our beach chairs as we watched our son, Seth, with his friend, who was a year older and half a foot taller, learning to skimboard. Skimming is a mix of surfing and skateboarding, but on the "skinny" water near the shoreline and, of course, without wheels. You run with your board in hand along the water's edge, release, and slide it in front of you so it glides across the glassy surface. You leap onto the board, now slipping along the placid water, and you're off. It's that simple—unless you're a middle-aged adult like me who hadn't skimmed in thirty years. Then, it's an ER visit in the making.

I had tried and failed a few times to show my son how to

skim before his older, taller friend, who had been swimming in the Gulf, revealed that he was a competent skimboarder (which would have been nice to know *before* my trinity of crashes into the surf).

His friend made it look simple. And really, it is simple. But it's not easy.

Seth failed numerous times. But he refused to quit, repeatedly trying, repeatedly failing. He grew dejected, frustrated, and I'm sure somewhat envious of his friend, who was skimming along swimmingly in front of me, my wife, our daughter, and some random guy with a Speedo, sunburn, back hair, and beer gut who kept reminding us how great at skimming he had been in his prime. He was an "I could've won state in skimming" sort of fellow.

"A little more like this," encouraged the friend, showing Seth how to slide the board in front of him without its nose burying. "And jump on the board more toward the middle-back. Keep trying, man. You'll get it."

That was the tip he needed—middle-back of the board. Within minutes, not only was Seth skimming but he was quickly outperforming his older friend. I expected this would annoy the friend, but instead, it seemed to please him. And he continued to encourage Seth.

They eventually tired of skimming and waded into the water and began to wrestle. My first instinct was to warn them to be careful, and by that, I mean I wanted to say to the friend, "Please don't hurt my son; you're taller and older."

But then again, I didn't want to embarrass my boy in front of his friend. So I let it play out.

Not to take anything away from Seth—he's a scrappy young buck who's strong and fast. I think he's part pit bull because he's ripped and doesn't have to work out. But his friend clearly had the advantage in the water, with the waves lapping over Seth's waist but cresting merely at his friend's thighs.

Seth lunged toward him, swinging himself around his taller friend and grabbing him from behind. They plummeted beneath the water, then cracked through the surface, shaking salt water from their eyes, cackling with laughter. Again and again, they repeated their match. Sometimes Seth got the best of him; sometimes his friend prevailed.

As the day progressed and the hot Florida sun reached its peak, an admiration for Seth's friend swelled in my heart, rising like the tide of those turquoise waters.

The friend could have overpowered Seth more than he did as they wrestled and slammed one another into the surf.

But he didn't.

And before that, he could have mocked Seth for each skimming crash.

But he didn't.

And he didn't not because he couldn't but because he wouldn't.

Because the older friend was meek.

You may have heard this line from a song: "Jesus, so lowly, meek, and mild."[1] Based on the company *meek* keeps in the lyric, sandwiched between *lowly* and *mild*, you may expect that *meek* means something like the way store-bought lettuce tastes—*meh*.

That's how I perceived the word *meek* on the rare occasion I came across it. To my mind, *meek* rhymed with *weak* and sipped afternoon tea with pastel virtues. Sissies are meek. *Real men* are not meek. And, most certainly, strong leaders are not meek.

But I had misunderstood meekness.

*Praus*—that's the Greek word for *meek*. It means something like *humble* and *gentle*.[2]

Now we know something of its formal definition. But while the definition is helpful, it doesn't help us fully understand what the word actually means.

Because dictionaries only go so far.

Take, for example, the word *fire*. You might look it up in a dictionary, and the definition seems obvious, familiar, and commonsensical. But if you were in my kitchen this morning as our teenager, Seri, cooked eggs before school and, with earbuds in, said aloud, "Bruh, this guy is *spitting fire*," you would wonder what on earth fire has to do with music. None of the dictionary definitions of *fire* have anything to do with singers spitting it. (In pop culture, apparently *spitting fire* means that a rapper is doing something *cool*—another word whose meaning transcends its most original literal definition.)

The context in which a word is used shapes its meaning. And this meaning evolves as time flows on.

So, yes, *meekness* means something like *humble* and *gentle*. But what does it mean when applied to Jesus in his first-century culture, and what does it have to do with Jesus' mindset as he resists the third temptation? And more than this, what does it have to do with our lives as we seek to follow the example of Christ?

+   +

In the ancient world, meekness was viewed as a disciplined calmness that a person with great power—someone like a king—should possess to govern effectively.[3] Meekness described the "self-discipline of an educated ruler who shows compassion for his subjects."[4]

And while it's true that *meekness* originated as a term to describe the most vulnerable in the ancient world—women, the poor, and slaves were considered *meek* because of their humble estate in life—it quickly gained traction as a virtue even the most noble and powerful hoped would come to describe their lives.

To be a meek ruler was to be a virtuous ruler. Why? Because the ancients discerned that those in authority needed meekness to harness or temper the power they possessed.

> In the ancient world, meekness was viewed as a disciplined calmness that a person with great power—someone like a king—should possess to govern effectively.

Viewed in this light, meekness would not have meant anything close to weakness as it pertained to rulers in Jesus' day. Quite the contrary. As author and speaker Dr. Mark Rutland notes, "Meekness is the supreme virtue of leadership without which power becomes tyranny."[5]

Meekness is the mother tiger scooping her young cub into her tenacious jaws and tenderly cradling its frail body, moving it from one place to another. Meekness is the martial artist who could destroy his unwitting, unskilled attacker but instead immobilizes him with minimal injury until authorities arrive. Meekness is the older, taller friend who could have crushed a younger boy's confidence but instead strengthened it.

Meekness is not the absence of power, but "power under control."[6]

So when Jesus turns to his mass of hearers hanging on his every word and teaches them, saying, "Take my yoke upon you . . . for I am [*praus*] and lowly in heart,"[7] they don't think that he's powerless. Remember, they'd all gathered precisely because of his power—to drive out demons, to heal the sick. He taught with an authority that defied the rabbinic leaders of his age.

When he invites them to bear his teachings, to take his yoke upon them, to believe that he is meek, they don't hear that he is impotent to effect change. On the contrary, what they hear is that he is a virtuous leader who, bearing power to work miracles and to befuddle the religious sages who contradict him, will not use his power to crush those who listen. They are in the presence of one who will not use his authority to disempower and oppress them. That kind of abusive power is what they'd come to expect from the powerful elites who ruled them.

But here was a man of meekness.

Here was a man with power under control.

---

They dragged her, perhaps naked and surely afraid, through the city streets. Her anxiety mounted as she approached the Temple—the epicenter of Jewish worship, the focal point of the law, the most powerful place in her world. She trembled at the thought of what awaited her—execution.

Early that morning, before her arrival, Jesus had left his perch on the Mount of Olives and had arrived at the Temple in order to teach. In the middle of his talk, religious leaders interrupted him and pushed forward the woman they'd apprehended.

"Teacher, this woman has been caught in the act of adultery. Now in the Law, Moses commanded us to stone such women. So what do you say?"[8]

The narrator reveals their motives, telling us they were using this woman's plight as a setup to test Jesus so that they might label him a heretic. They knew that Jesus would not execute her or condone her execution. They knew his temperament and had heard his teachings; this was simply a plot to expose him as a charlatan. They would entrap Jesus, who was teaching the law, by using the law against him.

The woman was their scapegoat, the law their sword. The gathered crowd provided witnesses but also evidence of why Jesus must be stopped—his ministry was gaining steam, a threat to the religious leaders' power and control.

So, while the woman is the central figure in the story, she's just a pawn in the hand of the law's power brokers.

They bring her and stand her before Jesus.

Jesus kneels before her, rubbing his finger on the earth and writing. We have no idea what he wrote. For that matter, we have no record that Jesus ever actually wrote anything other than these words or symbols, whatever they were.

Perhaps he wrote Leviticus 20:10, or maybe Deuteronomy 22:22, which would call for the discipline of both the woman *and* the man who were caught in adultery. But no man was apprehended. Or perhaps there was a religious leader in the group who himself was sleeping with her, and perhaps Jesus drew an arrow pointing to him, or for that matter, them.

Men wielded power over women. In many cases, women were treated as little more than property. And this is what makes the whole scene even more absurd—the law forbidding adultery, the law calling for the judgment of adulterers, is designed to protect the *property* of one man from being *stolen* by another. And so, the *man*, not the woman, who committed adultery would have borne the greater weight of offense—he was not just an adulterer but effectively was also a thief![9] But again, they're not concerned with the spirit of the law but its letter, written in stone like the rocks clutched in their hands.

Jesus stands, no longer kneeling, but now authoritatively facing the woman's accusers: "Let him who is without sin among you be the first to throw a stone at her."[10] In so doing, he offers all of them—offenders and defenders of the law—to see themselves in need of repentance, to see themselves as ones who have fallen short of the standard and missed the mark.

Because even as Jesus uses his power to confront them, he does so in hopes that those who are using their power to dominate and control will encounter true power, which offers them the possibility of redemption and repentance.

Jesus kneels before the adulterous woman.

And he writes.

He kneels and writes like the finger of God himself writing on tablets of stone.

And the woman's accusers drop their stones and leave, one by one.

And as she walks away, going to sin no more, perhaps his hearers and his disciples turn one to another and wonder whether this was what Jesus meant when he told that mass of humanity when they first began their journey together, "Take my yoke upon you . . . for I am [*praus*] and lowly in heart."

Having the power to condemn, Jesus uses his power to liberate—both the woman caught in the act of adultery and the men who'd dragged her into the Temple—if they were open to the freedom he offered.

> True power desires that none should perish, but that all would come to repentance and awaken to the path leading to life.

True power desires that none should perish, but that all would come to repentance and awaken to the path leading to life.[11]

This is the power of meekness.

In the third temptation, the devil offered Jesus the sort of power in an instant that would have sent him riding high through the Roman roads like Caesar himself. Instead, he chose the click-clack cadence of a donkey's gait as the pace of his leadership and ministry. "Behold, your king is coming to you, [*praus*], and mounted on a donkey."[12]

He could have wielded the power of the sword to overthrow his opponents; instead, in meekness he claimed the power of the towel and washed the feet of his followers, demonstrating to them that the greatest among them must "become as the youngest, and the leader as one who serves."[13]

He could have allowed the price of pigeons to inflate to match the size of the Temple money changers' egos, but in an act of meekness, he overturned tables and drove the extortioners from God's house with a whip.[14]

> *Meekness acts in power against anything that works toward separation—between God and humans, and between humans and one another.*

This doesn't sound like meekness, but it is. Meekness is not weakness and passivity. Meekness acts in power against anything that works toward separation—between God and humans, and between humans and one another.

Jesus had no shortage of opportunities to motivate the

masses, to whip them into a frenzy and set their hearts ablaze with hatred for their oppressors. But he knew that true power, the power of meekness, never seeks the domination of another. He knew that when you use power to control, not only do you diminish the other—made in God's image—but you also diminish yourself.

Jesus could have accepted a royal crown of splendor, but instead he chose a crown of thorns.

He could have turned stones to bread. He could have leaped from the Temple in an act of spiritual prowess. And he could have bowed before the devil and assumed absolute power in a moment. But he did not, because

> though he was in the form of God, [he] did not count equality with God a thing to be grasped, but emptied himself, by taking the form of a servant, being born in the likeness of men. And being found in human form, he humbled himself by becoming obedient to the point of death, even death on a cross. Therefore God has highly exalted him and bestowed on him the name that is above every name, so that at the name of Jesus every knee should bow, in heaven and on earth and under the earth, and every tongue confess that Jesus Christ is Lord, to the glory of God the Father.[15]

Let your attitude be the same.
Let your mindset be meekness.

# PRACTICE:
# WALK IN WORSHIP

RECENTLY, for the first time in over a decade, I had my eyes examined. Medicine labels had been giving me fits. Like a trombone player, I'd hold the bottle and then slide my arm further from and nearer to my body until the words came into focus.

"How about this one?" asked the optometrist, flipping a lens between my eye and a card with some tiny, blurry letters.

I focused, doing my level best to perform well.

"I can't read it."

"How about now?"

"Worse," I huffed. She then rapidly flipped lens after lens through the machine.

"Still no good . . . even worse . . . okay . . . little better . . . better . . . much better . . . holy cow! I can see it perfectly!"

*P-E-Z-O-L-C-F-T-D*—I blurted out the letters with the enthusiasm of an elementary student showing Mommy or Daddy how well the student can read!

It felt like an epiphany, yet it was just a piece of glass—a magnifier—that helped me see with greater clarity what was literally right in front of my face.

> *Worship is as much about awareness as it is about action.*

At a deeper level, I was having an actual epiphany. Earlier that day, I had been studying and thinking and writing about the topic of worship. And yet the more I wrote, the more I realized that you just can't explain to someone *how* to worship, as though it's a matter of following specific steps.

Because worship is as much about *how you see* as how you sing.

Worship is as much about *awareness* as it is about action.

But how do you teach awareness?

Articulating the mystery of what it means to experience God in worship feels like biting a wall[1]—the harder you try, the more you realize it's beyond your ability.

Maybe this is why the apostle Paul kept praying all the time for the church of Ephesus—that the Lord would open the eyes of their hearts, that they would see what other people could not see.[2] He knew that he could not open anyone's eyes.

But our eyes must be opened somehow to the nature and importance of worship. Worship is the practice that fosters a mindset of meekness and empowers us to resist the third temptation—to use power to control.

But I alone can't show you what you need to see about worship. Only the Spirit can open eyes. The best I can do is to sit with you and flip words on a page, pages in a book, and maybe one of these *lenses* provides a deeper sense of clarity about worship. Maybe one of them will even help you see worship from a fresh perspective.

✦ ✦

Face to face with the Ineffable on Mount Sinai as he received the law, Moses was transformed inside and out. Following this encounter, his skin was shining because he had been speaking with God, which struck fear in people when they encountered him.[3]

The ancient tradition tells us that this encounter caused Moses to become the meekest man in all the earth. And this meekness was never more apparent than when his power was later challenged by his closest relatives:

Miriam and Aaron spoke against Moses because of the Cushite woman whom he had married, for he had married a Cushite woman. And they said, "Has the LORD indeed spoken only through Moses? Has he not spoken through us also?" And the LORD heard it. Now the man Moses was very meek, more than all people who were on the face of the earth. And suddenly the LORD said to Moses and to Aaron and Miriam, "Come out, you three, to the tent of meeting." And the three of them came out. And the LORD came down in a pillar of cloud and stood at the entrance of the tent and called Aaron and Miriam, and they both came forward. And he said, "Hear my words: If there is a prophet among you, I the LORD make myself known to him in a vision; I speak with him in a dream. Not so with my servant Moses. He is faithful in all my house. With him I speak mouth to mouth, clearly, and not in riddles, and he beholds the form of the LORD. Why then were you not afraid to speak against my servant Moses?" And the anger of the LORD was kindled against them, and he departed.[4]

As the story unfolded, Moses did the opposite of what I would have done. I would have sat back and waited for my enemies to become my footstool. But Moses interceded before the Lord on their behalf, and the Lord relented.

At the very moment Moses could have felt compelled to establish his power, he instead prayed for the people who were threatening it.

> We don't need a holy mountain to marvel at the Almighty. We just need our eyes opened to walk in wonder in every moment, every day, wherever we are. Wonder is a gateway to worship.

Because Moses was disinterested in clamoring for control.

He had worshiped the Almighty on that mountain, and as the Ultimate Power overshadowed him in deep darkness, he saw his own power in the proper light.

Worship created in Moses a heart of meekness.

You and I will never scale Sinai and encounter the Lord like Moses did. However, the good news is we don't need a holy mountain to marvel at the Almighty. We just need our eyes opened to walk in wonder in every moment, every day, wherever we are. Wonder is a gateway to worship.

✦

Seri, maybe three years old at the time, stood in front of Elizabeth and me as we approached the next exhibit at one of the world's largest indoor aquariums. We stepped onto the conveyor belt, which pulled us into the glass tube. Water enveloped us on all sides, and rays of light pierced the deep blue veil, illuminating the brilliant hues of plants and sea creatures. The crowd hushed; hardly anyone moved.

We were seduced at a snail's pace into the abyss. I recall Seri's posture—the slight bend in her little legs, the backward tilt of her precious head, her transfixed gaze.

An enormous shadow swam into view and then glided above us. Seri smiled, not just with her mouth but with wide eyes and an astonished grin across her face as she watched the shark gracefully swimming overhead.

The group collectively gasped. Ambient music deepened the experience. The atmosphere was pregnant with a sense of the holy—time halting and thoughts fleeting as the moment baptized us in beauty.

"The shark gliding overhead is . . ."

The attendant's voice pierced the silence with the crackling, tinny tones of a microphone as she described the shark's species, size, home waters, and all manner of details.

I wanted to throw the stuffed whale that I overpaid for at the gift shop and pound my hands on the glass walls around me and stomp my feet and scream like a toddler: "I don't care! I don't care! I just don't care right this moment about anything you're saying!"

She was just doing her job. I get it. It wasn't her fault. And I didn't pitch a full-grown hissy fit. But in that moment, I just didn't care. It didn't matter to me the shark's size or species.

Because for a rare moment, my brain was not analyzing my experience in any perceivable way. It wasn't worrying or comparing or doing all the work it normally does to keep me safe and sane while simultaneously wearing me out.

For a moment, I wasn't trying to control anything. I was just drinking it in. I was saturated with wonder.

My heart throbbed with awe as I stood in that glass tube. I smiled and cried all at once. I was overwhelmed at the grandeur of God's creation. I wasn't just observing it; I was part of it, sucked away in the current of its magnificence.

Until words describing the moment shattered the silence in which we were all swimming, and the group began to point and murmur and ask stupid questions about the shark.

The holy dove flittered away as the shark swam out of view.

Some moments are better experienced than explained.

"Always we are chasing words," writes Heschel, "and always words recede. But the greatest experiences are those for which we have no expression. . . . Wonder alone is the compass that may direct us to the pole of meaning."[5]

Wonder—a characteristic of worship—is the way to answer the question at the heart of the third temptation, the question of meaning: *Do I matter?*

There is no pot of gold at the rainbow's end. There is no lasting sense of meaning found with the next promotion, the next milestone achieved, the next . . . whatever. Because the longing that led you to seek meaning in the *next* will remain when the *next* becomes *now*.

Wonder, however, invites you to see that all the meaning for which you long is embedded in this very moment.

Wonder is the ability to understand that while God is above all things—all things being created by him and for him—nevertheless, you can behold his presence running *through all things*.[6] As Wordsworth writes,

*A sense sublime*
*Of something far more deeply interfused,*
*Whose dwelling is the light of setting suns,*
*And the round ocean, and the living air,*
*And the blue sky, and in the mind of man,*
*A motion and a spirit, that impels*

*All thinking things, all objects of all thought,*
*And rolls through all things.*[7]

As we exited the tube, I wanted to go back inside—back into the stillness of a sacred moment. But time, like the conveyor belt that delivered us through the portal's other end, flows into the future. There was no going back into a moment. I would have to learn to experience that same sensation not only in carefully curated experiences but in the ebb and flow of ordinary life, rolling through all things.

I would have to learn to see the Great Mystery in faces and places far more familiar.

+

It was late in the summertime of 2020. School had recently commenced.

My son, Seth, age nine at the time, sat with me on our front porch. He was eating chicken tenders. I gazed into the canopy of pines across the street. It was a very normal moment, except the circumstances were unusual: He was quarantined due to being infected by the COVID-19 virus.

"Seth, it's crazy to think that something unseen, a microscopic virus, can have such a huge impact," I commented.

"Yeah, Dad, it's just that there's so much of this very small thing in the world."

"I know, Son. There's so much of so many things in this world that we cannot see."

"Dad, I think that there's more that we cannot see than what we can see. What do you think?"

"Yeah, buddy, I think you're right. And I think that we hardly see the things that we can see because we're not paying attention. But if we saw everything God sees, we'd be overwhelmed."

"And that's why he's God, Dad."

We sat for a moment. My vision blurred as I gazed at a pine, taller than the rest, swaying in the distance.

Seth spoke tenderly. "Hey, Dad, thanks for everything you do for our family."

"Thanks for noticing, Son," I replied. "That means a lot."

He was paying attention.

He knew that his being home, being quarantined, had disrupted my routine. He knew that I could not work and write and go about my daily assignments as usual. And somewhere amid doctor's visits and nasal swabs and being reminded to drink ever more fluids, he saw something—he saw *me*. I'm not sure when he saw me; I wasn't aware of the moment, but it became apparent when he said, "Thanks for everything you do for our family."

He saw what I can only describe as *the thing behind the thing*. He saw love. He saw a father's devotion. And I could never teach him how to see this. He just had to pay attention, to notice.

I'm pretty poor at this practice. I often don't pay attention. I don't often notice.

Because I'm busy.

Because every moment for me is just an echo of a previous moment—I've seen it all before—and I'm constantly comparing everything that is to what has been.

I hardly hear the words that people speak because I think I already know what they're going to say.

I cannot remember whether my father, whom I just saw last week, has a clean-shaven face, a goatee, a mustache, or a beard. Seeing him, I hardly *see* him. Because he's familiar.

And yet I have friends who would give their life savings for just one more moment to study the face of a deceased loved one. They'd stare into their eyes, they'd spread their hands across that delicate space between cheekbones and temples, and they'd *see* them as if for the first time, for the last time.

They'd behold them with wonder.

*Walking in wonder is not about seeing miracles that blow your mind. It's about being mindful enough to see miracles in the most ordinary, everyday moments of life.*

Walking in wonder is not about seeing miracles that blow your mind. It's about being mindful enough to see miracles in the most ordinary, everyday moments of life. As Rabbi Steinsaltz wrote,

If I am ready for miracles, I can walk down the street and see sunshine, and that is enough of a miracle. If I am not ready for miracles, seeing thirty dancing angels will not do anything to me.[8]

It's about paying attention. It's about slowing. It's about noticing. It's about being open to the possibility that the whole of creation is shot through with Divine Presence, and that all things exist in God and by God and for God.

That all things—though they're not God—can point us to God.[9]

You are part of something deeply meaningful. You are a participant in God's ongoing creation, a creation that he *spoke* into existence, but which Scripture tells us that he *saw* was good.[10]

God *saw* that it was good—perhaps because it was too good to describe with words.

And we, like God, need to *see* its goodness.

To see the Unseen in everything we can behold.

We need to walk in wonder so that we can worship God, not only on this mountain or that mountain, as Jesus taught us, but rather in spirit and in truth[11] as we wander through life's valleys and even through our own backyards, city streets, and home hallways.

Let us have eyes to see. Let us slowly, daily walk the trail of wonder and arrive *at the pole of meaning*. Let us marvel at the grandeur of God's good creation. Let us gaze, as if for the first time, into the eyes of our children, our lovers, our fathers, and our mothers. Let us stare into the pines and flowers until our eyes mist over and our hearts expand, and we behold that all things are knit together by the thread of Divine Presence.

"When the LORD your God brings you into the land that he swore to your fathers," Moses, mouthpiece of God, spoke to the people, "then take care lest you forget the LORD, who brought you out of the land of Egypt, out of the house of slavery. It is the LORD your God you shall fear. Him you shall serve and by his name you shall swear."[12]

Moses' words embolden Jesus as he faces his final temptation: to bow down and worship the devil in exchange for the power to control.

"Be gone, Satan!" Jesus says authoritatively. "For it is written, 'You shall worship the Lord your God and him only shall you serve.'"[13]

And with this, the temptations conclude.[14]

But not forever, as Luke tells us, filling in details that Matthew spares his readers. No, "when the devil had ended every temptation, he departed from him *until an opportune time*."[15]

There would come many moments throughout Jesus' life and ministry when he'd be seduced to strive, perform, or control in some form or another.

And he'd resist them all.

But for now, the temptations ceased, and he rested.

And angels drew near and ministered to him.

Then he emerged from seclusion and walked among the people. He drove out demons with a word, healed the sick who touched the fringe of his garments, and opened blinded eyes. How? Luke tells us that when he completed his temptations, he "returned in the *power* of the Spirit."[16]

Not the power of the world, but the power of the Spirit.

Not the power of the devil, but the power of the Spirit.

Not the power to control, but the power of the Spirit.

It was the Power who had brooded over the chaotic deep in Genesis, which brought order to chaos.

It was the Power who thundered at Sinai.

It was the Power who lighted on Jesus at his baptism.

It was the Power who would show mercy to the vilest of sinners.

It was the Power who would come to sustain Jesus and lead him every day of his life.

And in the end, it was this Power who would raise him from the dead.

And so it will be for us.

So let us worship the Lord our God and serve him only.

# TO THE END

*Now before the Feast of the Passover, when Jesus knew that his hour had come to depart out of this world to the Father, having loved his own who were in the world, he loved them to the end. During supper, when the devil had already put it into the heart of Judas Iscariot, Simon's son, to betray him, Jesus, knowing that the Father had given all things into his hands, and that he had come from God and was going back to God, rose from supper. He laid aside his outer garments, and taking a towel, tied it around his waist. Then he poured water into a basin and began to wash the disciples' feet and to wipe them with the towel that was wrapped around him.*[1]

Some parents tell their children at bedtime, "I love you to the moon and back."[2] They're not saying to the child, "If my love for you were measured, the distance of my love for you would be 477,710 miles."[3] No, they're saying to the child, who cannot fathom the distance from her little bed to the moon, that they love her more than she can imagine.

I wonder what the Gospel writer is trying to communicate when he writes that Jesus "loved them to the end."[4] In this story, often referred to as the Last Supper, Jesus nears the culmination of his time together with his disciples. Maybe the Gospel writer is being literal by saying that Jesus loved them from the time he met them until the end of their time together—start to finish he loved them.

Or maybe the Gospel writer is saying something like the parent to the child at bedtime, that Jesus loved them to the end, to the full extent of his love for them—he loved them with all he had. He'd spent over three years cultivating friendships with them, teaching them, and making memories with them. He'd loved them from the first moment he laid eyes on them, and now he was loving them "to the end," to the full extent of his love for them.

Or perhaps both are true—having come to the end of his earthly time with them, he loved them to the full extent. Whatever the case, the action that demonstrates his love for them is the same: He stands from supper, removes his outer garments, ties a towel around his waist, pours water into a basin, washes their feet, and wipes their feet with the towel.

It's hardly the farewell speech, the climactic moment, that you'd expect from a leader of his caliber. This was the man who'd raised the dead, performed unfathomable miracles, defied the wisdom of religious leaders, resisted every temptation, and passed every test that came his way. This was not what you'd expect from someone of Jesus' stature and status. But here he was, the man who'd risen to the highest heights in their hearts and minds, bowing to the lowest depths and washing their feet.

Why is this the lasting memory he desired to imprint in their minds? Why foot washing at a meal? Because this was the type of people he wanted them to become—the type who loved other people as he loved them, as he served them.

*This was the type of people Jesus wanted his disciples to become—the type who loved other people as he loved them, as he served them.*

this was the type of people he wanted them to become—the type who loved other people as he loved them, as he served them. It's this sort of love that would reveal to the world the love of God; it's this type of love that would reveal that they were Jesus' disciples.[5]

As Jesus loved them, they were to love the world.

As Jesus loved them, we are to love the world.

When you really think about the way that Jesus loved them, how he offered his time and attention to them, how he sacrificed his life so that they could find the meaning of theirs, how he resisted the power of the sword and took up the power of the towel, you scratch your head and wonder, *How is this sort of love even possible?* And then you find yourself helpless, incompetent, and—in your own strength—powerless to love others with that sort of love.

How did Jesus love like this? How are we to do the same?

The Gospel writer hid the answer in plain sight: "Jesus,

knowing that the Father had given all things into his hands, and that he had come from God and was going back to God, rose from supper."[6]

> When you know where you've come from and where you're going, then you live a different sort of life.

Jesus knew where he had come from and where he was going.

When you know where you've come from and where you're going, then you live a different sort of life. You don't strive through life, grinding it out; you trust. You don't perform for approval; you gratefully receive your identity from God. You don't dominate and control others with power; you serve in meekness.

Jesus knew where he had come from and where he was going.

Do you?

How do you see your life? Is it a haphazard blip between your birth date and funeral? Or was your life dreamed up in the heart of the divine and knit together in your mother's womb with creativity, compassion, and care? Are you spiraling headlong toward an uncertain future, or are you carried along by the One who sees you, the One who has always seen you, the One who will hold you in his heart for eternity?

When you know where you've come from and where you're going, daily temptations toward security, approval, and power to control all pale in comparison to the reality that you are a child of God. God will provide for you, God approves of you, and God has invested you with holy power to serve the world.

And now we've arrived at the real question. The question that answers all the other questions. The question that calls for striving, performing, and controlling to cease. The question behind the questions.

Where have you come from and where are you going?

This is the real question that calls us to question ourselves, God, and others, *Will I have enough? Am I enough? Do I matter?*

Where have you come from and where are you going?

You've come from God, and you're returning to God. And if the life and ministry of Jesus teaches us anything, we can be sure of this: Along the journey, God is with us all the way through, and he loves us to the end.

# Reflection and Discussion

1. Has there been a time when you felt like Hagar, running *from* something but not knowing what or where you're running *to*?

2. Reread the descriptions of the three temptations outlined on page 15-16. With which do you most struggle? Why?

3. Slowly read Matthew 3:13–4:11. Immerse yourself in the scene as you watch John baptize his cousin Jesus. Hear the Father speak those beautiful words to Jesus. See the Spirit descend like a dove. Then read the passage again, noticing any thoughts, emotions, or images that emerge. Take a moment to write or discuss what strikes you about this scene and your responses to it. How does it make you feel? What stands out to you?

4. Allow the words that the Father spoke over Jesus to apply to you. Feel free to revise the phrasing a bit if it helps. *[Your name], you are my daughter/ son. I love you. I'm well pleased with you.* Remember and recite these words, especially when you are discouraged.

5. What stands out to you about this chapter?

CHAPTER 2
—————

1. In what areas of your life do you most feel the need to prove yourself?

2. Do you struggle with the idea that God is well pleased with you? Why or why not?

3. Think back to your early days growing up. How do you think your relationship with your parental figure(s) shaped how you view your relationship with God?

4. In what ways do you think you've been offered shortcuts to a truly meaningful life? How did these shortcuts prove unfulfilling?

5. Based on what you've just read, what gives you hope?

6. What stands out to you about this chapter?

## CHAPTER 3

1. What do you need to release and receive?

2. In what ways do you feel like you will not have enough (time, money, etc.)?

3. Think about the idea of *kavanah*, or intention. Why is *kavanah* such an important factor in how we go about our lives and work?

4. In what areas of your life does it feel like you're trying to fly a kite without wind?

5. What stands out to you about this chapter?

## CHAPTER 4

1. Has there been a time when your trust in God was shaken? If so, what was that like for you? If not, how do you imagine you'd feel in that situation?

2. How can the sense of God's absence actually be a gift or invitation to you?

3. Why do you think some Christians look down on questioning God or bringing difficult questions to him?

4. If your trust in God deepened, what about your life would change?

5. What stands out to you about this chapter?

CHAPTER 5

1. Prior to reading this chapter, how did you think about Sabbath? What thoughts or emotions did your reading evoke in you?

2. What's one thing you rarely or never get to do that is life-giving or enjoyable?

3. Put yourself in the sandals of an Israelite. What about the manna-gathering rhythm would be difficult for you?

4. Have you ever thought about rest as a holy assignment? How does this concept shape your view of Sabbath?

5. What stands out to you about this chapter?

CHAPTER 6

1. How has our culture contributed to the prevailing need to perform for approval?

2. In what area of your life do you find yourself most often performing for approval?

3. What voice in your head (a former coach, colleague, parent, boss, pastor, relationship, etc.) makes you feel like you are not enough? Can you state the lie and then state the truth?

4. What stands out to you about this chapter?

## CHAPTER 7

1. Is your outlook on life one where you focus on problems or on blessings?

2. Do you view everything as a gift? Why or why not?

3. Who is the most grateful person you know, and why do you consider them grateful?

4. What's one step you can take to practice gratefulness?

5. What stands out to you about this chapter?

## CHAPTER 8

1. When you hear the word *meditation*, what comes to mind?

2. Why do you think many are skeptical of meditation?

3. Is it easy or challenging for you to meditate on Scripture? Why or why not?

4. How does Scripture meditation make us more grateful?

5. What stands out to you about this chapter?

## CHAPTER 9

1. Recall the best boss and the worst boss you've ever had. What makes each one stick out in your memory? What separates them from each other?

2. Power has garnered a bad reputation. How can power be a good thing?

3. What is the long-term impact of using power to control, versus using power to uplift and serve? You might think about your response in terms of this playing out in the workplace, at school, at home, in a relationship, etc.

4. What stands out to you about this chapter?

## CHAPTER 10

1. How have you previously understood the meaning of *meekness*?

2. How does seeing meekness as *power under control* shape your understanding of it?

3. Does it bother you that only the woman caught in the act of adultery was brought before Jesus to presumably be executed? Why or why not?

4. Henri Nouwen wrote, "What makes the temptation of power so seemingly irresistible? Maybe it is that power offers an easy substitute for the hard task of love. It seems easier to be God than to love God, easier to control people than to love people."[1] What resonates with you about this statement?

5. Why do you think that the way Jesus related to power disappointed some people who had other expectations of him?

6. What stands out to you about this chapter?

## CHAPTER 11

1. How would you define *worship*?

2. How does worship create in us a mindset of meekness?

3. Describe the most holy moment you can recall. Where were you? How did you feel?

4. How is wonder a vital element in worship?

5. What stands out to you about this chapter?

## EPILOGUE

1. How would you answer the question *Where have you come from and where are you going?*

2. Now that you've read the book, which of the three temptations—to strive for security, to perform for approval, or to control through power—do you most struggle with, and why?

3. What questions remain for you?

4. What stands out to you about this epilogue?

# Acknowledgments

You would not be reading this book if John D. Blase from The Bindery Agency had not believed in it and helped it find a home at NavPress. He is one of my favorite writers, and I'm still shocked that I get to call him my agent.

The team at NavPress offered not just publishing expertise but hospitality and friendship. I'm grateful to David Zimmerman for his support of this book, and to Caitlyn Carlson and Elizabeth Schroll for their editorial efforts. I'd list all the things I appreciate about their abilities, but I'd spend too much time stressing over whether I should use semicolons or commas.

Numerous friends and colleagues read drafts of the manuscript throughout the years and provided thoughtful feedback. Among them are: Dr. Austin Carty, Owen Stone, T.J. Shaffer, Sheena Ratliff, Gileah Taylor, Luke and Kera Williams, Jody and Kristi Mann, Jenna and Zach Gibson, Kelly and Chris Brown, Brent and Emily Jennings, Austin Bailey, and Lauren Daley.

Pastor Phil Daniels and Generations United Church have given me the privilege to work in a church where I'm able to write and teach. Before these words found their way onto the pages you're holding, they were spoken and discussed with disciples in our congregation. I hope the interactions these ideas generated helped us all mature in Christ.

Seri and Seth, my children, are in many ways my text. I see God at work in their lives, and I hear God speaking through their words. I wrote this book so that they'd know how their father—full of faults and prone to error—nevertheless followed Christ the best he knew how. I hope these words provide for them a trail to follow.

Elizabeth, my wife, walked with me as a faithful companion through the high points and lows of every sentence in these pages.

Finally, Rabbi Arthur Kurzweil has been a source of friendship and wisdom—an answer to prayer, a gift from the Almighty.

# Notes

CHAPTER 1 | THE THREE QUESTIONS WE'VE ALWAYS ASKED

1. Genesis 12:2; 13:16; 15:5. The rest of the story transpires throughout chapter 16.
2. Inspired by Sheryl Crow's "Soak Up the Sun" (*C'mon, C'mon* © 2002 A&M Records): "It's not having what you want, it's wanting what you've got."
3. Dallas Willard wrote, "Familiarity breeds unfamiliarity—unsuspected unfamiliarity, and then contempt." *The Divine Conspiracy: Rediscovering Our Hidden Life in God* (New York: HarperCollins, 1998), 11.
4. This is how the ESV footnote for Genesis 16:13 translates the verse according to the Hebrew.
5. It is apparent from the passage that not all the temptations transpire in the wilderness. However, over time, this series of temptations, which began in the wilderness, became known as the "wilderness temptations," to differentiate them from the other temptations Jesus faced throughout his life and ministry.
6. Rainer Maria Rilke, *Sonnets to Orpheus* with *Letters to a Young Poet*, trans. Stephen Cohn (Manchester: Fyfield Books, 2006), 212.
7. I picked up this phrase from Rob Bell on his podcast, *The Robcast*.
8. Fyodor Dostoevsky, *The Brothers Karamazov*, trans. Richard Pevear and Larissa Volokhonsky (New York: Farrar, Straus and Giroux, 1990), 252.
9. Ruth Haley Barton, *Life Together in Christ: Experiencing Transformation in Community* (Downers Grove, IL: Intervarsity Press, 2014), 30. Barton is summarizing the writings of Thomas Keating from *The Human Condition: Contemplation and Transformation* (New York: Paulist, 1999).
10. Eric E. Peterson and Eugene H. Peterson, *Letters to a Young Pastor: Timothy Conversations between Father and Son* (Colorado Springs: NavPress, 2020), 82.

11. The order of the Temptations differs in the narratives provided by Matthew and Luke. Mark offers an account of the wilderness temptation but affords no specifics regarding the content of the three temptations. John omits the wilderness temptation narrative altogether. For the sake of clarity, I will only reference the account in Matthew, unless otherwise noted. Among my reasons for selecting Matthew's version are the account in Mark provides none of the dialogue between Jesus and Satan, and the account in Matthew is considered by most scholars as nearer to the original than Luke's. See Birger Gerhardsson, *The Testing of God's Son (Matthew 4:1-11 & PAR): An Analysis of an Early Christian Midrash* (Eugene, OR: Wipf and Stock, 2009), 11.

### CHAPTER 2 | THE FOUNDATION OF IDENTITY

1. A form of the Greek root word *peirazō* is translated as *tempted* in Matthew 4:1. According to New Testament scholar Jeffrey Gibson, "The evidence indicates that it was basically the idea of being *probed and 'put to the proof'*, that is, 'tested' *to ascertain or to demonstrate trustworthiness.* And when the participle [*peirazō*] . . . was used . . . with reference to a person, its connotation was even more specific: *being probed and proved, often through hardship and adversity, in order to determine the extent of one's worthiness to be entrusted with, or the degree of one's loyalty or devotion to, a given commission and its constraints.*" Therefore, it is appropriate to think of the Temptations as tests or trials to prove Jesus' fidelity to God. Jeffrey B. Gibson, *The Temptations of Jesus in Early Christianity*, Journal for the Study of the New Testament Supplement series 112 (Sheffield, England: Sheffield Academic Press, 1995), 56-57.

2. According to Birger Gerhardsson in *The Testing of God's Son*, "The theme 'Son of God' was deeply rooted in the traditional religious ideology of Israel. It was a favourite variant of the election and covenant themes . . . ; for many centuries Israel had been accustomed to thinking of herself as a chosen people, and as God's covenant people and as God's son" (21). Scripture abounds with references of Israel as God's son: Exodus 4:22; Deuteronomy 1:31; Jeremiah 31:9; and Hosea 11:1, to name a few.

3. Gibson, *Temptations of Jesus*, 98.

4. Romans 12:2, NIV.

5. In Galatians 4:5, Paul reminds the church that they have been adopted as God's children, and in 4:19 that Christ is being formed in them.

6. Matthew 7:14.

7. Eugene H. Peterson, *A Long Obedience in the Same Direction: Discipleship in an Instant Society* (Downers Grove, IL: InterVarsity Press, 1980).

8. Matthew 3:17.
9. While Jesus is the only begotten Son of God (John 3:16), all who believe and have received Jesus are "[given] the right to become children of God" (John 1:12).

CHAPTER 3 | TEMPTATION: STRIVE FOR SECURITY
1. Matthew 4:2-4.
2. Luke 2; Matthew 2:13-23.
3. Luke 2:41-52.
4. Leonard Sweet and Frank Viola, *Jesus: A Theography* (Nashville: Thomas Nelson, 2012), 86.
5. Sweet and Viola, *Jesus: A Theography*, 97.
6. The idea of the possibility that Jesus had to provide for his family as a laborer comes from Sweet and Viola, *Jesus: A Theography*, 97.
7. Exodus 12:40.
8. Exodus 16:3.
9. Matthew 4:4.
10. *Turned water to wine*: John 2:1-12. *Multiplied bread and fish*: Matthew 14:13-21; 15:32-39; Mark 6:30-44; 8:1-10; Luke 9:10-17; John 6:1-14.
11. 1 Samuel 16:7.
12. John 5:19-20.

CHAPTER 4 | INVITATION: CHOOSE TO TRUST
1. John 6:1-25.
2. John 6:25-35, 53-57.
3. John 6:67-69.
4. "Dark night of the soul" is often translated as the title of a sixteenth-century poem by St. John of the Cross, "Oscura Noche" (Dark Night).
5. Julian of Norwich, *Revelations of Divine Love* (Mineola, NY: Dover, 2006), 48.
6. Romans 8:28.
7. It was Arthur Kurzweil who remarked to me, "Trust is knowing God is, like I know my body is. I don't wonder about my body; it just is."
8. John 8:28-29.
9. Deuteronomy 8:3.
10. Pastor Helmut Thielicke said a similar phrase in his book *The Silence of God* (Grand Rapids, MI: Eerdmans, 1962), 9. He writes: "We do not know what will come. But we know who will come. And if the last hour belongs to us, we do not need to fear the next minute."

CHAPTER 5 | PRACTICE: REST IN SABBATH
1. Exodus 16:4-5, 17-30.
2. Lynne M. Baab, *Sabbath Keeping: Finding Freedom in the Rhythms of Rest* (Downers Grove, IL: InterVarsity Press, 2005), 52.
3. Genesis 2:1-3.
4. A Jewish Sabbath prayer attributed to Chaim Stern in Central Conference of American Rabbis, *Mishkan T'filah: A Reform Siddur*, ed. Elyse D. Frishman (New York: CCAR Press, 2007), 81 and 688.
5. *Tanakh—The Holy Scriptures: The New JPS Translation According to the Traditional Hebrew Text* (Philadelphia: The Jewish Publication Society, 1985), 3.
6. Genesis 1:27.
7. My friend was paraphrasing something Abraham Joshua Heschel wrote in *The Sabbath: Its Meaning for Modern Man* (New York: Farrar, Straus and Giroux, 1951), 32. Quoted in Baab, *Sabbath Keeping*, 55.
8. Baab, *Sabbath Keeping*, 45.
9. Baab, *Sabbath Keeping*, 45.
10. See Luke 6:1-11; 13:10-17; 14:1-6; John 5:1-17; 9:1-41.
11. Baab, *Sabbath Keeping*, 46.
12. Matthew 12:8.
13. Baab, *Sabbath Keeping*, 46.
14. Isaiah 58:13-14.

CHAPTER 6 | TEMPTATION: PERFORM FOR APPROVAL
1. Matthew 4:5-6.
2. Birger Gerhardsson, *The Testing of God's Son (Matthew 4:1-11 & PAR): An Analysis of an Early Christian Midrash* (Eugene, OR: Wipf and Stock, 2009), 56-58.
3. Thrice-annual pilgrimages to the Temple in Jerusalem (for Passover, the Feast of Weeks, and the Feast of Booths) were commanded in the Torah. For more on this topic, see Rabbi Daniel Kohn, "What Are Jewish Festivals?" My Jewish Learning, accessed February 17, 2023, https://www.myjewishlearning.com/article/pilgrimage-festivals/.
4. Luke 2:41-52.
5. Matthew 4:6.
6. Psalm 91:1, 7.
7. Psalm 91:11-12.
8. Matthew 4:7.
9. Exodus 17:1-7.

10. Psalm 95:9.
11. Matthew 4:7.

## CHAPTER 7 | INVITATION: OPEN YOUR HEART IN GRATITUDE

1. Alan Morinis, *Everyday Holiness: The Jewish Spiritual Path of Mussar* (Boston: Trumpeter, 2007), 64.
2. Brother David Steindl-Rast, *Gratefulness, the Heart of Prayer: An Approach to Life in Fullness* (New York: Paulist Press, 1984), 12.
3. Psalm 95:7-9, emphasis mine.
4. *The Book of Legends (Sefer Ha-Aggadah): Legends from the Talmud and Midrash*, ed. Hayim Nahman Bialik and Yehoshua Hana Ravnitzky, trans. William G. Braude (New York: Schocken Books, 1992), 77.
5. As quoted in Summer Allen, PhD, *The Science of Gratitude*, White Paper, The John Templeton Foundation, Greater Good Science Center at University of California, Berkeley, May 2018, https://thegratitudeconcept .com/wp-content/uploads/2018/10/GGSC-JTF_White_Paper-Gratitude -FINAL.pdf, 8, 38.
6. Allen, "The Science of Gratitude," 28-35; and Diana Butler Bass, *Grateful: The Transformative Power of Giving Thanks* (New York: HarperOne, 2018), 29.
7. Joan Moran, "Pause, Reflect and Give Thanks: The Power of Gratitude During the Holidays," (UCLA, October 29, 2013), https://newsroom .ucla.edu/stories/gratitude-249167.
8. Robert Emmons, "What Gets in the Way of Gratitude?" *Greater Good* Magazine, November 12, 2013, https://greatergood.berkeley.edu/article /item/what_stops_gratitude.
9. "Parshat Lech Lecha In-Depth: Genesis 12:1–17:27," Midrash Rabbah; Tosefot Shantz, Sotah 10a. See https://www.chabad.org/parshah/in-depth /default_cdo/aid/35872/jewish/Lech-Lecha-in-Depth.htm.
10. Morinis, *Everyday Holiness*, 67. Rabbi Bachya ibn Pakuda, an eleventh-century Jewish philosopher, identified these three reasons in *Al Hidayah ila Faraid al-Kulub* (*Duties of the Heart*).
11. Viktor E. Frankl, *Man's Search for Meaning* (New York: Pocket Books, 1985), 86.
12. Steindl-Rast, *Gratefulness*, 80.
13. Ephesians 5:20.
14. Quoted in a personal email from Arthur Kurzweil on October 31, 2021.
15. Colossians 1:16.

16. Luke 24:16.
17. Luke 24:30-31.
18. Luke 24:35.
19. Numerous writers and speakers have illustrated this point, but I first encountered it in "Being the Beloved," a sermon by Henri Nouwen, which I found at https://www.youtube.com/watch?v=trG7Oh_PopM.

CHAPTER 8 | PRACTICE: MEDITATE ON SCRIPTURE

1. Matthew 4:5-7, emphasis mine.
2. Matthew 12:34-35.
3. Donald S. Whitney, *Spiritual Disciplines for the Christian Life*, rev. and updated (Colorado Springs: NavPress, 2014), 46.
4. Psalm 1:1-2.
5. Thomas Merton, *Contemplative Prayer* (New York: Image Books, 1971), 67.
6. Alan Morinis, *Climbing Jacob's Ladder: One Man's Journey to Rediscover a Jewish Spiritual Tradition* (Boston: Trumpeter, 2002), 90.
7. John Ortberg, *The Life You've Always Wanted: Spiritual Disciplines for Ordinary People* (Grand Rapids, MI: Zondervan, 2015), 188.
8. As quoted in Ortberg, *The Life You've Always Wanted*, 186. Emphasis added.
9. Eugene H. Peterson, *Working the Angles: The Shape of Pastoral Integrity* (Grand Rapids, MI: Eerdmans, 1993), 88.
10. Peterson, *Working the Angles* (Grand Rapids, MI: Eerdmans, 1993), 103.
11. Matthew 2:15.
12. Genesis 37 begins the account of Joseph's time in Egypt, and Exodus 1 begins the account of Israel's struggles in Egypt.
13. I attribute this phrase to my friend John R. Bost, who told me that when he reads the Bible, it reads him at the same time. In recent years, I've seen this phrase appear in various other writings, though my usage of it is based on John's comment and any potential similarities to other writers is coincidental.
14. Numerous resources exist online. For starters, here is one that covers *lectio divina* and gospel contemplation: https://www.ignatianspirituality.com/ignatian-prayer/the-what-how-why-of-prayer/praying-with-scripture/.

CHAPTER 9 | TEMPTATION: CONTROL THROUGH POWER

1. Abraham Joshua Heschel, *The Sabbath: Its Meaning for Modern Man* (New York: Farrar, Straus and Giroux, 1951), 3.
2. Matthew 4:9.

3. The story begins in Exodus 19, leading to the golden-calf incident in Exodus 32.
4. Exodus 32.
5. Exodus 20:3.
6. Matthew 4:10.
7. Genesis 3:5.
8. Colossians 1:16.

## CHAPTER 10 | INVITATION: SEEK TO BE MEEK

1. The Angelic Gospel Singers, "Glory, Glory to the Newborn King," recorded 1950, side A on *Glory, Glory to the Newborn King / Jesus Christ Is Born*, Gotham-G-675, 1950, 78 rpm. Authorship of this song has been disputed, but according to an article in *The Canterbury Dictionary of Hymnology* and at this link (https://www.hymnologyarchive.com/jesus-oh-what-a-wonderful-child), Margaret Wells Allison composed the song and the lyrics. This song is often referred to by its first line: "Jesus, oh what a wonderful child." The version of the song being referenced here was recorded by Mariah Carey in 1994 on the album *Merry Christmas* (Legacy Records).
2. *The UBS Greek New Testament*, 4th rev. ed. (Stuttgart: Deutsche Bibelgesellschaft, 2010), 151*.
3. Deirdre J. Good, *Jesus the Meek King* (Harrisburg, PA: Trinity Press International, 1999), 7.
4. Good, *Jesus the Meek King*, 87.
5. Mark Rutland, *Character Matters: Nine Essential Traits You Need to Succeed* (Lake Mary, FL: Charisma House, 2003), 109.
6. Rutland, *Character Matters*, 109.
7. Matthew 11:29.
8. The whole scene transpires in John 8:1-11.
9. Gail R. O'Day, "John," in *The New Interpreter's Bible Commentary Vol. 9* (Nashville: Abingdon Press, 1995), 628.
10. John 8:7.
11. 2 Peter 3:9.
12. Matthew 21:5.
13. Luke 22:26.
14. John 2:13-17.
15. Philippians 2:6-11.

## CHAPTER 11 | PRACTICE: WALK IN WORSHIP

1. Abraham Joshua Heschel, *Man Is Not Alone: A Philosophy of Religion* (New York: Farrar, Straus and Giroux, 1979), 30.

2. Ephesians 1:18-19.
3. Exodus 34:29-35.
4. Numbers 12:1-9.
5. Heschel, *Man Is Not Alone*, 15-16.
6. Colossians 1:16-17.
7. William Wordsworth, "Lines Written a Few Miles above Tintern Abbey," in *Lyrical Ballads: 1798 and 1802*, with Samuel Taylor Coleridge (Oxford: Oxford University Press, 2013), 89.
8. Adin Steinsaltz, *Simple Words: Thinking About What Really Matters in Life* (New York: Touchstone, 2001), 206-207.
9. Romans 1:19-20.
10. Genesis 1:31.
11. John 4:21-24.
12. Deuteronomy 6:10, 12-13.
13. Matthew 4:10.
14. For Matthew, the temptation of power to control is the final temptation. For Luke, it is the second temptation.
15. Luke 4:13, emphasis mine.
16. Luke 4:14, emphasis mine.

EPILOGUE | TO THE END
1. John 13:1-5.
2. The origin of the phrase is unknown according to https://www.dictionary.com/e/slang/love-moon-back/ (accessed August 26, 2022).
3. The moon is an average of 238,855 miles away, so a trip there and back would traverse 477,712 miles.
4. John 13:1.
5. John 13:34-35.
6. John 13:3-4.

REFLECTION AND DISCUSSION
1. Henri J. M. Nouwen, *In the Name of Jesus: Reflections on Christian Leadership* (New York: Crossroad, 1989), 77.

**NavPress is the book-publishing arm of The Navigators.**

Since 1933, The Navigators has helped people around the world bring hope and purpose to others in college campuses, local churches, workplaces, neighborhoods, and hard-to-reach places all over the world, face-to-face and person-by-person in an approach we call Life-to-Life® discipleship. We have committed together to know Christ, make Him known, and help others do the same.®

Would you like to join this adventure of discipleship and disciplemaking?

- Take a Digital Discipleship Journey at **navigators.org/disciplemaking**.
- Get more discipleship and disciplemaking content at **thedisciplemaker.org**.
- Find your next book, Bible, or discipleship resource at **navpress.com**.

 @NavPressPublishing

 @NavPress

 @navpressbooks